D0030927

ZEN
TEEN

ZEN TEEN

40 WAYS TO STAY CALM WHEN LIFE GETS STRESSFUL

TANYA CARROLL RICHARDSON

SEAL PRESS

Copyright © 2018 Tanya Carroll Richardson

Hachette Book Group supports the right to free expression and the value of copyright. The purpose of copyright is to encourage writers and artists to produce the creative works that enrich our culture.

The scanning, uploading, and distribution of this book without permission is a theft of the author's intellectual property. If you would like permission to use material from the book (other than for review purposes), please contact permissions@hbgusa.com. Thank you for your support of the author's rights.

Seal Press
Hachette Book Group
1290 Avenue of the Americas, New York, NY 10104
www.sealpress.com
@sealpress

First Edition: September 2018

Printed in the United States of America

Published by Seal Press, an imprint of Perseus Books, LLC, a subsidiary of Hachette Book Group, Inc. The Seal Press name and logo is a trademark of the Hachette Book Group.

The Hachette Speakers Bureau provides a wide range of authors for speaking events. To find out more, go to www.hachettespeakersbureau.com or call (866) 376-6591.

The publisher is not responsible for websites (or their content) that are not owned by the publisher.

Print book interior design by Trish Wilkinson

Library of Congress Cataloging-in-Publication Data
Names: Richardson, Tanya Carroll, 1974– author.
Title: Zen teen: 40 ways to stay calm when life gets stressful / Tanya Carroll Richardson.
Description: Boston: Seal Press, [2018] | Audience: Age: 12 and Identifiers: LCCN 2018007877| ISBN 9781580057820 (pbk.) | ISBN 9781580057837 (ebook)
Subjects: LCSH: Awareness—Juvenile literature. | Self-consciousness (Awareness)—Juvenile literature. | Resilience (Personality trait) in adolescence—Juvenile literature.
Classification: LCC BF311 .R4877 2018 | DDC 155.5/19—dc23
LC record available at https://lccn.loc.gov/2018007877

ISBNs: 978-1-58005-782-0 (paperback), 978-1-58005-783-7 (ebook)

LSC-C

10 9 8 7 6 5 4 3 2 1

CONTENTS

INTRODUCTION

Hello! Tanya Carroll Richardson here, the author of this book. Although I hesitate to call myself the author because so many of the concepts in *Zen Teen* are drawn from ancient wisdom that has been updated, by myself and many others, to fit our modern times.

As I write this note, I'm in my early forties (I know that seems *incredibly* old to you right now, but when you get to be my age it won't seem so old, and you will realize that in many ways you're still the same person you were at seventeen). I've learned a couple of things for sure about the pressures and challenges of everyday life. I feel confident that when I share what I've learned with you, you can experience new levels of peace and lasting happiness so that when you face a setback, detour, or disappointment, you will feel more prepared to overcome it. You're already stronger and more capable than you know. (This is a wonderful lesson life teaches us all.) My hope is that this book will help you be more open to joy during the good times and more resilient when life is (really, really) hard.

The year I turned eighteen was probably the most challenging time of my life, and I admit I felt very lost. My mother died when I was seventeen, and my last two years of high school I didn't concentrate on schoolwork. In fact, I found out on the final day of high school that I had failed a chemistry course and wouldn't graduate with my class. That same week, I had to get an apartment and a job and start life on my own as an "adult." To make matters even more challenging, I had developed an eating disorder my senior year of high school and wasn't physically or emotionally healthy. I got through it with the help of loud music and good friends, and some of the practices you'll find in this book. By learning how to manage stress and overcome anxiety, I eventually took a summer course to finish high school, enrolled in college, and went on to get a master's degree. I moved to London and then New York City, where I have worked as a writer for twenty years. I am married to the love of my life, and I can truly say that I am mentally and physically healthier (and happier) than I ever thought possible during my teen years.

I wish I'd had a book like *Zen Teen* in my life back when I was struggling with intense emotions and anxiety about the future. But since I don't have a magic time machine to take me back so I can tell my eighteen-year-old self all these mindfulness practices (wouldn't that be cool?), I did the next best thing: I wrote them down in a book for you.

Your life might be going great right now, and if it is, good for you! For those of you who feel the powerful pressure of everyday realities, I get it. The goal of this book is to show you how to make the most of the good times, help you find more meaning in each day, and teach you to navigate the stressful moments and challenging emotions we all sometimes experience. You can't always change what happens to you, but you can change your reaction to what happens and learn coping skills to make the best of any situation.

Somehow life has magically sent me everything I needed to face my challenges. The tools in this book should help you meet your own challenges.

As a teen, you need extra love, gentle support, and an optimistic attitude. Most of all, you need to stay mindful. That will help you cultivate more calm and claim more confidence. Life is an adventure, and I want yours to be inspiring, exciting, and full of assurance that you are ready for whatever comes.

Love,
Tanya

WHAT IS MINDFULNESS?

A ll the sections in this book have one thing in common—
they each encourage you to be more mindful. Doctors,
CEOs, athletes, actors, and teachers are always talking about how
mindfulness changes health, businesses, performance, the creative
process, and lives. But if you asked 100 people who practice mindfulness to tell you exactly what mindfulness *means*, you would
probably get 100 different answers. Annoying, right? Sometimes
it's really comforting to know that 2 + 2 = 4!

It's pretty funny that everyone has their own ideas about what
mindfulness means because the whole point of mindfulness is to
simplify life. Less confusion, less drama, less stress. But stick with
it because when the concept becomes clear, everything else will,
too. You might think of mindfulness as cleaning out the closets
of your mind. Or you could picture a garden that is overrun with
weeds, and think of mindfulness techniques as the tools that help
you trim those weeds back.

You know that relaxed, accomplished, peaceful feeling you get
when you walk into a room that used to be messy and is now clean
and tidy? That's the same feeling mindfulness brings.

Mindfulness is about creating space in our minds and our lives,
some breathing room for pauses, rest, and reflection. More of the

good stuff that helps us mindfully craft our lives—just like a potter crafts a wet lump of clay into a beautiful bowl—so we are happier and calmer and feel like we have some control in navigating our journey. Every exercise in this book is designed to make you more mindful. Just as you developed healthy habits when you were a kid, such as learning how to share or brushing your teeth, you can also develop the habit of mindfulness now as a teen.

If you did ask 100 people what mindfulness is, what are some of the typical answers you might receive? Mindfulness could be described as being in the moment, being purposeful, being present, being nonjudgmental, being self-reflective. It's all those things. Most of all, though, mindfulness is about being aware—aware of what is happening right now, aware of your thoughts, aware of the possibilities, and aware of any patterns in your life you would like to change or end altogether.

Instead of being at the mercy of your thoughts, emotions, negative patterns, or life in general, mindfulness returns control to you. Of course, we can't control *everything*. The weather is a great example: we can't control whether it rains or not. But there's a big difference between being caught outside in a thunderstorm and being caught outside in a thunderstorm with an overcoat, an umbrella, and a cool pair of rain boots. Mindfulness lets you walk through your days with all the gear you need to handle even life's thunderstorms in relative comfort.

When it comes down to it, it doesn't matter what mindfulness means to other people. This book is about giving you the tools to decide what mindfulness means for *you*. And that is exciting. Because teens like you are at a magical, powerful age, an age where you finally have the freedom to:

Design your own unique life so you can live at your highest potential.

Decide what is important to you and where you want to focus your time and energy.

Figure out what it all means and discover your own personal philosophy on life.

Determine how you will approach the highs and lows, the challenges and the victories, of your journey.

Learn about what brings you peace and joy. Some of these are universal (like love), and some are specific to each individual (like which flavor of ice cream you want in your sundae—one of life's most important questions).

These choices can come with challenges, and those challenges can bring about feelings of fear, panic, stress, depression, and anxiety. You know what I'm talking about because you've been there—we *all* have. Don't give up or lose hope just because life becomes challenging—instead, approach the tough times with mindfulness, and you'll find those negative feelings becoming more manageable. That makes room for fun feelings like peace and excitement.

Think of this book as your mindfulness buffet. If a concept or exercise works for you or resonates, put it on your plate. If something you read or try does not feel like a fit for you and your world, just move on. But while you are reading this book, stay open and curious. Sometimes the things you never thought you'd like on a buffet turn out to be what you go back for again and again.

Each concept in this book has its own special section. Within each section you'll find a breakdown of why the concept works, the philosophical (or super wise and intellectual) reason this concept is special, a practical approach so you can start using this concept in everyday life, the shadow side or negative aspects of this concept to watch out for (this can stop you from misapplying a concept or taking a concept too far), and the magical (or almost unbelievably cool) parts of the concept. Each concept will come with straightforward tips and exercises to help you better under-stand and practice this mindfulness technique.

Have fun with this book. Some things you study you might never use again in real life. But mindfulness is a subject you can apply to any aspect of your life and use again and again.

PART 1

Meditation, Mantras & Making Peace with Life

Set Intentions

Why it works: Setting an intention—an aim, a plan, or a desire—gives you some control over your existence by choosing a direction to head in. It's like plugging a destination into the GPS of life so it steers you toward where you want to end up: *I will introduce myself to the new kid who moved in down the street. I will play a gig in public with my band. I will get a great summer job.*

Intentions can also be about feelings, like: *I will be brave in class. I will be patient during soccer practice. I won't let someone else's silly or rude behavior get to me.*

An intention doesn't guarantee you will reach your ideal destination, but it's a powerful first step of exercising your free will instead of unconsciously letting life happen to you.

A philosophical perspective: Intentions are where everything new begins. Do you have a dream? It began with an intention. Do you have a goal? It began with an intention. The more you gently focus on an intention, by reminding yourself of it daily, the more likely you will be to manifest the outcome you desire.

Make it work for you: Intentions work best when they are flexible. When an intention faces a roadblock, don't give up—just redefine the goal. Let's say your crush can't attend a concert with you. Instead of thinking "my intention to go with my crush failed," revise your intention to a goal that you can reach: "I'll go to the concert with a friend and have fun no matter what." That allows you to change your approach and still get something you want—an awesome, memorable concert experience. Staying flexible is one of the mindfulness keys to success and happiness in life, so stay flexible with your intentions, too!

The magical side of intentions: Magic happens when we interact with life and become a co-creator of our destiny. Setting an intention is the simple but powerful act of putting words to what you want. And if things don't work out exactly as planned, you will still get closer to your goal if you aim mindfully at your target with an intention.

The shadow side of intentions: To everything in life, there is a shadow side. You might think of a shadow as dark, negative, challenging, or an opposite. The shadow side of setting an intention is this: intentions do not guarantee outcomes. After all your best efforts (studying hard, working with a tutor, turning in your homework on time), you still might end up with a disappointing grade in chemistry. That's why one of the most powerful intentions you can set is, "I will always try my best and be proud of my effort." Or, how about: "When things don't turn out as I hoped, I will be kind to myself."

Give it a try: For one week, set a single positive intention each morning before you leave the house. Here are a few you can borrow:

1. "I will seek out the simple pleasures in life today."
2. "Kindness is a gift I will give to myself and others today."

3. "I'm going to fake it until I make it today and approach life with confidence."
4. "Today I'll show compassion to my favorite person and be very gentle with myself."
5. "I'll come up with a mini goal today to aim for in the future."
6. "Today I will concentrate on what I like most about myself."
7. "I want to challenge myself today to stretch in a new direction."
8. "Today I will face one of my fears."
9. "Being healthy is my focus today."
10. "Today I just want to have fun and savor the moments."
11. "I really want to chill today and not take anything too seriously or too personally."
12. "Today I'll see how many people I can make smile or laugh."
13. "Today is about quiet time and recharging my batteries, so I'm avoiding unnecessary stress and drama."
14. "Instead of concentrating on what I want to change about my life, today I'll focus on what I'm grateful for."
15. "I'll try something new today, even if it's something small."
16. "Today I'll tell someone I trust about what is upsetting me or ask someone supportive for help."

2

Get Some Gurus

Why it works: When you focus your attention on someone you admire by observing their character traits and behaviors, you are better able to emulate the values that person embodies. But you don't just *observe* their wisdom, you take it in and make it your own. The guru's wisdom is imparted not just through the guru's words and actions, but via their very essence.

What is a guru?

"Guru" is a Sanskrit word that dates back to early Vedic Hindu texts. In India, gurus are guides or masters who other people follow, study, or emulate. In *Star Wars*, Yoda acts as Luke Skywalker's guru, teaching him the ways of the Force. In the Christian tradition, Jesus Christ, followed by a band of disciples called apostles, could be considered a guru.

A philosophical perspective: We all need people to look up to, people to learn from. Another word for guru is "mentor"—someone you respect and want to be more like. Mentors teach simply by setting an example you can follow with confidence.

Mentors and gurus offer us collective wisdom so we can all be better people and work toward becoming the best versions of ourselves. One day, someone you know might look to you as a guru or mentor—or perhaps people already do, whether you are aware of it or not!

Make it work for you: A guru doesn't have to be famous, just enlightened. And you don't have to tell your guru that you look up to them. Just observe your gurus and learn by watching how they take on situations and challenges. If someone you admire is famous, you can read their books, study their career, and learn about their earlier life. It's especially helpful to find someone to look up to who excels at something you would like to improve in your own life—like your relationships, your hobbies, or your studies.

The magical side of gurus: Gurus inspire greatness! Our hearts, minds, and souls crave fresh experiences and philosophies, and gurus give them to us by offering windows into exciting new worlds. Gurus are everywhere and easy to find: in fact, some may come onto your radar almost by magic, just when you need someone to show you a new way.

The shadow side of gurus: Gurus are still human, and therefore they can be wrong and make mistakes. No one is perfect. Look up to your gurus, but try not to idolize them. Your goal is not to *become* your guru, but to learn from your guru so you can be a better, more unique you. Also, no single person has all the answers, so you don't have to be loyal to just one guru. Instead, you can have several at a time, and you will probably switch gurus many times throughout your life as you change, grow, and develop new needs and dreams.

Give it a try: You can choose as many gurus as you want, but start by selecting one. When you've chosen your guru, write in your journal or on a piece of scratch paper about why you admire this person. Find a picture of your guru and put it up in your room, locker, or somewhere you will see it often. Take notice of the guru's value as a role model: What specifically can this guru inspire you to do, understand, change, or improve?

Tips and tricks:

Pick someone you like a lot, even if you don't know why. Someone's subtler traits can inspire you to live your best life.

Choose someone in a field or career you're interested in pursuing, or with a talent you hope to develop. This person can be working in their field today or be someone from history.

Keep in mind that your gurus don't have to be real people. Do you have a favorite character from a book or movie? This character can become a guru.

Expand your observation by identifying reasons you admire this person that have nothing to do with their job, talents, or skills.

Look beyond your gender, interests, and day-to-day routine to find role models you admire. You may not have much in common with a guru to begin with, which can expand your horizons or worldview.

Don't overlook people you know well or see every day as guru candidates. Classmates, relatives, and teachers make great gurus because you can observe them up close.

Find your guru! Here are a few famous ones to consider:

Amandla Stenberg

Amy Purdy

Beyoncé

Elizabeth Gilbert

Ellen DeGeneres

Emma Watson

Greta Gerwig

GT Dave

Janis Joplin

Jazz Jennings

John Green

Justin Trudeau

LeBron James

Mahatma Gandhi

Malala Yousafzai

Marie Curie

Martin Luther King Jr.

Michelle Obama

Misty Copeland

Neil deGrasse Tyson

Neil Patrick Harris

Oprah Winfrey

Tina Fey

3

Journal for Answers & Wisdom

Why it works: When you get stressed, emotions build up inside that make you feel overwhelmed and confused. Journaling releases this pent-up energy and helps you mindfully process these feelings so they become more manageable and eventually pass.

Keeping a journal is not only a way to keep a record of your life, it's also a way to express your hopes, challenges, feelings, and passions. There are no rules with journaling: You can write as much or as little as you want. You might go for weeks without picking up your journal, and then suddenly find yourself writing in it every day. Your journal is a safe place where you can be yourself with no fear and express your hidden thoughts and emotions. Looking back over old journal entries will allow you to see patterns in your life—the positive ones you will want to repeat, and the negative or self-sabotaging ones you want to change.

When you're journaling, be sure to write down your biggest victories, recording how people congratulated you or supported and helped you achieve this win. This will solidify the victory in your mind and memory and give you faith that more triumphs will follow.

Likewise, journals are an excellent place to explore your disappointments. Writing about a missed opportunity or a friendship that didn't turn out the way you expected can help you sort out your feelings. Emotions like anger and sadness can be hard to sit with. Putting them on paper can let you identify the lessons they have to teach you, and then move beyond them so you can feel peaceful and happy again.

A philosophical perspective:
Journaling is a wonderful way to make sense of life and connect with your higher self—that part of you that's very wise and insightful. There are many answers already inside you, but sometimes you need to go deep to find them. Writing helps you tap into that deeper, inner self, the part of you that can offer a fresh perspective.

Make it work for you:
This might sound obvious, but be sure to keep your journal in a very safe place where it won't get lost, damaged, or read by other people. Storing your journal at school or in another public area is probably a bad idea—even the idea of someone else finding it and reading your most private thoughts can keep you from being truly free with your writing. Keep your journal in a private spot—in your desk at home or a bedside drawer, where it is out of sight. Don't tell anyone else where your journal is, so you can have peace of mind that it's private. You can also use an online journal that is password-protected. If someone else finds and reads your journal it's not the end of the world, but your journal is really meant to be a safe place where you can have private conversations with one of your favorite people—yourself!

The magical side of journaling:
When you write in your journal, know that life is listening! If you're mad at someone, let it out in

your journal. Getting angry is healthy and natural, and your journal is a safe place to take out all that aggression. And if you want something really, really badly, write about it—when you write about your deepest wishes and those things you yearn for most, you'll find that life will listen. It may even send you messages back, by giving you ah-ha ideas about how to reach your goals or putting you in the path of golden opportunities.

The shadow side of journaling: Over time, your journal should become a trusted confidant. But remember to share your feelings and ideas with your friends and family, too. Sometimes all you need a friend or family member to do is just listen and let you know that they care. Try not to write about things in your journal only from your perspective, but use your heart and your higher self to help you see a situation from all sides and understand other people's true motivations.

Journaling tips:

Don't put any pressure on yourself to "be a good writer." Spell things wrong, leave sentences incomplete, and don't even worry about making paragraphs. You can't journal "wrongly," and journaling should never feel like a chore. Let yourself free associate with phrases and ideas, draw pictures, create lists, and otherwise jot down whatever comes to mind.

Give it a try: Go out and buy a journal this week. It doesn't have to cost a lot of money, but make sure you like the way it looks on the outside. You can always decorate the cover of your journal with pictures, fun colors and patterns, inspiring words, or drawings. Inside, make sure the journal has plenty of room for you to fill it with all your memories, feelings, life lessons, hopes, and goals.

Here are some prompts to get you started:

I loved it today when . . .

This week was hard because . . .

Something I want to change about my life is . . .

Someone who has become very important to me is . . .

I got angry when . . .

This was a huge disappointment for me . . .

I'm really excited that I'm making steady progress on . . .

It may have happened a long time ago, but I'm still upset about . . .

One of my biggest victories recently was . . .

Something I'm afraid of that's giving me anxiety is . . .

I want to do more nice things for myself, like . . .

I always feel calmer when . . .

Doing this is guaranteed to make me smile or laugh . . .

Right now, my most cherished dream in life is to . . .

Something I've been procrastinating about that I know I need to get started on is . . .

This really surprised me, and I'm not sure what to think about it or what it means . . .

Only recently did I figure out what my true motivation was behind . . .

I got mad at a friend today, but later I realized I was really upset about . . .

Today I realized that I have a pattern of behavior that I want
    to change . . .

Someone said something really interesting to me today . . .

This week I experienced some intense emotions, and I want to
    make sense of them . . .

I feel like it's time to ask for help with . . .

I've waited long enough, and I'm finally ready to . . .

I discovered something I didn't realize I was talented at . . .

I saw something amazing today, and it's inspired me to . . .

A friend said one thing to me today, but I think what they
    really meant was . . .

Today I heard/read something that was so wise . . .

4

Master Meditation

Why it works: Turning your mind's volume down is the ultimate stress buster.

Some of the earliest mentions of meditation are in sacred Indian texts known as Vedas, written in Sanskrit thousands of years ago. A loose definition of meditation could be an attempt to quiet, still, or focus the mind. If you've taken a yoga class, your instructor probably asked you to assume corpse pose toward the end, close your eyes, and meditate. The goal was to make your mind blank or calm.

Meditation slows down the constant chatter and internal monologue that go on inside our heads. A calm mind means a calm nervous system, which means less anxiety and more feelings of peace and tranquility. The more you get in the habit of meditating—maybe for fifteen minutes as you get ready in the morning or while you are browsing for clothes in a store—the more your mind will get used to the idea of being silent or at rest.

Brains, like the muscles in our body, can be trained. So, when you make meditation a regular practice, your mind will be more still and calm even when you aren't meditating. If you are one of the many people who've had problems with anxiety in the past, meditation can be a wonderful tool. Another way brains are similar to other muscles is that they require rest. Sleep and meditation are perfect ways to give your mind a nap.

A philosophical perspective: This jumble of thoughts that are racing, repetitive, or excessively negative is what Buddhists call "monkey mind"—a mind that resists being tamed. Philosophers from thousands of years ago, like Buddha, and modern-day thinkers, like Eckhart Tolle, believe that there is deeper peace and wisdom underneath or beyond the chatter of the monkey mind.

Make it work for you: Have you ever heard the phrase *everything in moderation*? That includes meditation, too. If you like to sit in the lotus position and meditate for hours, props to you. But just setting the intention to meditate for ten minutes once a day can bring amazing results. And if you skip a day or two of meditating? No worries. Just get back to it as soon as you can.

The magical side of meditation: Besides helping to calm the nervous system and control anxiety, meditation makes room in the mind for the important thoughts. So much of what runs through our minds are the same thoughts we have over and over, or fear thoughts. When you consciously make your mind quieter, the important thoughts stick out. Thoughts that let you know how you really feel about something or someone, ah-ha ideas that bring you new solutions to old problems, words of wisdom from your soul, and messages of love from your heart.

The shadow side of meditation: Meditation, like anything else, takes practice before you can get great at it. The aim is not to stop all thoughts coming into your mind, but to make them fewer and create more blank space in between these thoughts. If you feel like meditation is challenging for you, be gentle with yourself and keep trying.

Give it a try:

Step 1. Pick one of the methods of meditation on pages 18–20.

Step 2. While meditating, make a conscious choice to slow and deepen your breaths.

Step 3. Now try to observe how much space is in between your thoughts. At first you probably won't be able to notice *any* space between your thoughts. Keep playing with it until you do notice space, and then try to make that space longer and longer.

Step 4. Keep at this exercise, and you'll be surprised at how much space you can create between your thoughts. This is meditating!

Tips and tricks:

Make your meditation practice your own. You might like to begin by striking a singing bowl or ringing a bell, or by playing a favorite song that inspires you and brings you a feeling of calm. You could spray a scent into the air for aromatherapy or cover your eyes with the hood of a soft sweatshirt to block out distractions. You might hold your favorite pillow or fold a cozy, warm blanket and sit on top of it or stretch out underneath it. Do whatever makes you feel comfortable and makes meditation something you look forward to.

What type of meditator are you?

Everyone's meditation "practice" will be unique. To find what works for you, take note of any activity that allows your mind to become calm and still. Such as:

Walking meditation: A popular practice among Native American tribes and Aboriginal tribes of Australia. The theory being that repetitive movement can help calm or still the mind. This is not limited to walking, and includes jogging, yoga, and dancing. A great excuse to have a dance party (hey, I'm trying to meditate here), it explains why people feel so free and happy when dancing! Their minds are quiet.

Creative meditation: Being immersed in a creative project like writing, sewing, or painting can quiet the mind. This might help explain why artists are so passionate about and devoted to their work—it's relaxing. Develop a creative hobby as a stress-buster for your brain.

Everyday meditation: Believe it or not, you can practice meditating while performing everyday activities like doing chores, cooking dinner, or riding the bus. This is in fact the goal, to be able to quiet your mind anytime and anywhere. Often while we are engaged in other activities we are on autopilot—instead of letting your mind wander, try to keep it quiet and see what important thoughts rise to the surface.

Traditional meditation: This is what most people think of when they think of meditation: sitting cross-legged on the floor with their eyes closed. Some people find this a very soothing, natural way to meditate. Others find it

What type of meditator are you?

more challenging or intimidating. Give traditional meditation a try and see how it feels to you.

Breath-work meditation: A form of meditation that is becoming more and more popular—concentrating on the breath to calm the mind. When the body is getting plenty of oxygen it naturally relaxes (this is why, although it's probably your natural instinct, you should not hold your breath or take short, shallow breaths when you are stressed). Some people like to take very long, deep breaths, being mindful of when they breathe in and out. However, there are many variations on breath-work meditation. Check out others online.

Visualization meditation: Do you like movies or photography? Maybe you are a visual artist or just love beauty. If so, you might picture a color, landscape, crystal, animal, or other visual image in your mind while you meditate. You could even meditate on an image of yourself or your life as you would like it to be. Find an image that is calming and positive.

Guided meditation: This is where you listen to someone talking you through the meditation. These are usually prerecorded, and the person guiding you might be telling a story or giving you specific images or words to concentrate on while you close your eyes and listen. It's a very powerful practice and a great way to dig deep into your mind for wisdom. There is usually a specific goal with this type of meditation, such as uncovering patterns in your life you may not be aware of.

Sound meditation: It can help for the mind to have something gentle to focus on during meditation, like the sound of rain, a gong, low chanting, or your favorite soft, easygoing song. When the mind can settle on

continues

What type of meditator are you?   *continued*

calming background noise you can often trick it into calming down. Try using nature sounds, a white noise machine, or gentle music.

Nature meditation: Research shows that being in nature has a relaxing effect on the nervous system. Spending time in nature is a proven stress reliever, and when we are less stressed it's easier to calm the mind and meditate. Nature certainly has a strong energy that brings us back to life's natural rhythms and helps us stay focused on the present moment instead of fretting about the future or analyzing the past. Go out into nature, even if it's just your backyard or a local park, and see how that energy affects your own.

5

Use the Power of Realistic Optimism

Why it works: Practicing "realistic optimism" keeps you from going into fear-based or worst-case-scenario thinking.

We each often have a "default mode," or a natural state we return to again and again. Some of us might be pessimists, always anticipating the worst—*I'll probably get an F on that test; I'm sure I'll be lonely after transferring schools.* An optimist is someone who is always expecting the best—*Our garage band is going to get a major label deal; I bet I'll get into an Ivy League school with a full scholarship; I'm going to have a first kiss with my crush on Valentine's Day with fireworks going off in the background!*

Somewhere in the middle, between deep pessimism and grandiose optimism, is realistic optimism.

Being "real" means you don't shy away from the facts of a situation. A **realist** acknowledges there is a problem. A **realistic optimist** envisions the best possible outcome and does what she can to make it come true. A **realist** who is only a sophomore trying out for the varsity basketball team acknowledges there are players who are older and more experienced. A **realistic optimist** decides to try out anyway, hoping for a chance to play, and also to watch, learn, and improve for next year.

A philosophical perspective: Positive thinking is powerful. It encourages people to be hopeful about situations and work toward happy outcomes. However, positive thinking alone cannot change a situation. And there are some situations that, no matter how positive an attitude we bring to them, will still not work out the way we want. Realistic optimism is a grounded way to stay positive, where you acknowledge all the challenges and negative aspects of a situation while still hoping for and working toward some sort of happy or peaceful ending.

Make it work for you: If you are shopping for an attitude or philosophy to adopt for the long haul, realistic optimism is as solid as they come. It sets you up for success because you will always be looking on the bright side and hoping for the best while still being present to what is, or the hard facts of a situation (just like a detective looks at the facts of a case). Realistic optimism is not only positive, it's practical. Because it leans toward optimism, adopting this attitude is a great way to check yourself when you have become too pessimistic or sad about something, someone, or life in general.

The magical side of realistic optimism: When you're feeling optimistic, you are more open, which means it will be easier for you to spot possibilities that others might overlook or discount, and then draw these opportunities to you. Realistic optimism also gives you a magical dose of energy or stamina so you can keep going when the going gets tough.

The shadow side of realistic optimism: Sometimes even the most realistic of hopes can be dashed. Talk to friends, family, and experts when you are facing a tough or intimidating situation. And don't beat yourself up if you get down or feel pessimistic.

Everyone does sometimes. It might mean that you simply need to acknowledge you are feeling sad, angry, or frustrated about a situation. All normal stuff.

Give it a try: Choose a situation or relationship that doesn't feel as good as it could. Imagine a pleasant or peaceful outcome and focus on that vision. The way we think about things can be very habit forming, so if you've been feeling pessimistic, it may take a little time before optimism feels natural. Every new habit takes practice! When you train yourself to have an optimistic attitude, you will feel lighter, happier, and more satisfied with what life offers you.

Tips and tricks:

Step 1: Identify the unavoidable and difficult truths about a situation.

Step 2: Identify your biggest hopes and expectations for the situation.

Step 3: Put both perspectives in a mental blender and hit pulse. Taking both the challenges and opportunities into account, what is the best *realistic* outcome?

Step 4: Take action steps that will lead you closer to that result.

Step 5: Stay positive throughout the process and adjust your definition of "realistic" as conditions change.

Create Space

6

W hy it works: Modern life can be hectic no matter what your age, so getting in the habit now of creating space—building time into each day to breathe, chill, reflect, and play—can be an important tool you'll use throughout your life. School, work, chores, sports, clubs, hobbies, and family obligations are all valuable pursuits, but can take an enormous amount of energy and time. To stay calm, it's important to schedule free space into your day, with no agenda. You can use that time however you like: reading, fiddling with a creative project, or recharging with a hike outdoors.

A philosophical perspective: Have you heard the expression "less is more"? When people study philosophy, they are seeking a way to get more out of life—a path to a fuller, richer human experience (and by studying *Zen Teen* you are doing just that). Yet sometimes the way we actually get more out of life is by doing less, working less, and thinking less.

Make it work for you: There's always more you can do in life. If you aren't careful, "doing" will fill every minute of your waking time. Creating space protects you from accidental overload, which can cause anxiety, and saves room for reflection, rest, and spontaneity.

The magical side of creating space: During the space in be-tween activities, new dreams and desires will call to you. Some-times the hardest part of finding happiness is answering the question, "What makes me happy?" When you have space in your life you're in touch enough with yourself to know or discover the answers to that important question.

The shadow side of creating space: Resist the urge to fill your space with an activity. The point of downtime is to allow it to be flexible and free-flowing. If you want to use that time to shoot hoops with a friend, awesome! But don't do it because you feel obligated or pressured—this is time reserved for *you*.

Give it a try: This week, find a way to fit forty-five minutes of space into one of your weeknights (Monday through Friday), and an hour and a half of space into the weekend (Saturday or Sun-day). Book this time as solid, uninterrupted blocks. For this ex-ercise, designate one of these space times to be spent hanging out alone and off the computer.

Tips and tricks:

In the beginning, you'll probably have to consciously plan extra space into your schedule until your body and mind get used to this new rhythm.

The space you create can be as short as twenty minutes. Look for available pockets of time, like before you start getting ready in the morning or at night after your homework, chores, or job are finished.

Learn to say "no" to things you don't want to do or don't have to do.

Take time away from your phone, television, and computer.

Create space while you're out and about—take the scenic route somewhere instead of the fastest route.

Savor your meals. Plan a healthy meal that you have to prepare and then take your time eating it. This helps your body learn to slow down.

Spread out activities instead of planning them back-to-back.

Go outside at night in a safe place, like your backyard. Spread a blanket in the grass and stare up at space for a while.

Arrive to events fifteen minutes early and spend that time not on your phone but in quiet contemplation. You'll be surprised what insightful thoughts pop into your head!

7

Make Mantras That Calm You Down & Build You Up

W hy it works: Self-talk is the stuff we all say to ourselves in our minds. The most important things we say all day are what we say to ourselves, the things that no one else can hear. Mantras insert positive ideas into our self-talk.

Do you ever pay attention to how you talk to yourself in your head? Maybe you catch yourself thinking, *No one ever takes my side at home.* Or if you're struggling trying to learn a new language, instrument, or sport, you might tell yourself silently, *I'm just useless! I'll never get this.* When you have a thought cross through your mind that you don't like, stop and gently check yourself. It's negative self-talk, and you probably love yourself a whole lot more than your brain just made you believe. Tune into your heart for the real answer: *I'm not good enough* could become a mantra like *I'm a great person and I'm doing the best I can.*

A philosophical perspective: Mantras can change the way you approach situations and look at people—including yourself. The right mantra can change the world, because it can change you. In truth, you affect everyone and everything you interact with.

Make it work for you: Mantras can act as life preservers when you're drowning in stress. They also provide a way out of a negative self-talk pattern that, like any pattern, will only get stronger or worse until you begin shifting it. Changing negative self-talk will improve your self-confidence and your mood. If negative self-talk is a real problem for you, base a significant amount of your mantras on self-love. "I'm awesome," "I'm flawsome" (awesome even with all your flaws—we *all* have "flaws"), "I just get better and better every day," or "I love myself no matter what" are great, simple self-love mantras.

The magical side of mantras: Mantras are especially good at helping you find your center again when intense emotions make you feel stormy. When you first wake up in the morning can be a very stressful time, as you might begin running through the to-do list of everything you have to accomplish that day, and for most teens that's a lot: school, part-time jobs, extracurricular activities, chores, and homework. A great morning mantra is: "My day unfolds naturally with plenty of time to get it all done." You can repeat this mantra throughout the day if you're feeling overwhelmed. This mantra can magically change your mood. You will still have the same amount to accomplish, but you will approach the day not stressed but calm, which will magically change the way you experience the day.

The shadow side of mantras: Life is always changing, and sometimes your mantras need to change, too. You might have some favorite mantras you use your whole life, but if you want to rework a mantra or change it altogether, you are the boss. Mantras should feel authentic and inspiring. If you have a mantra like, "I'm happy and easygoing," but you keep feeling down and anxious, try something more specific to overcoming what you're feeling, like "This will get better."

Sample mantras:

"I'm a unique person who was put on this earth for a special reason."

"I have a big heart, which people love about me."

"I look for the opportunity in setbacks."

"I stand up for what I believe in."

"I find ways to diplomatically speak my mind."

"Asking for help when I need it is a sign of strength."

"I always find time to take good care of myself."

"My good deeds magically come back to bless me."

"I always bounce back from disappointments."

"I spend time on what is most important to me."

"The friends I bring into my life value me and treat me well."

"I don't sweat the small stuff."

"Believing in myself creates miracles."

"I always have my own back."

"I'm easygoing like Sunday morning."

"I make choices that help me live at my highest potential."

"I do my best to be kind to everyone."

"I'm not perfect but I learn from my mistakes."

"I treat others as I would want to be treated."

continues

Sample mantras   *continued*

"When something bad happens, life balances it with something good."

"I enjoy becoming friends with people from different backgrounds so I can expand my worldview."

"Cool, interesting stuff is always happening to me."

"Somehow things always work out in the end."

"Amazing people and opportunities come into my life."

"I extend grace and mercy to myself and others."

"Life is a sacred adventure."

Give it a try: Pick one of the mantras from pages 29–30 or make up a mantra of your own, and use it in your thoughts regularly for a week. Notice the changes in your mood, behavior, self-love, and self-confidence.

Tips and tricks:

The more often you use a mantra, the more powerful it becomes, because in time your subconscious mind will incorporate the mantra and you'll experience less random, negative self-talk popping up in your brain. You can think your mantras anytime you want, but it will be even more effective if you write them down—in the margins of your notebooks, in your journal, or on a sticky note you post to the bathroom mirror.

8

Color Your Mood

Why it works: Scientists have proven that many people have an emotional response to color. Colors are stimulating—they engage our senses and make us feel more alert, calmer, and even happier. A room that is all beige (furniture, walls, art, etc.) can be boring or understimulating, which can make humans feel cranky, tired, and even stressed. Colors invoke associations and encourage particular moods, often in very personal ways. For instance, forest green might remind you of the woods and fairies, so when you're surrounded by green, you feel a sense of freedom and playfulness.

Imagine you're walking into a room that's painted in a soft, warm pink. Can you feel it? Now, imagine walking into a room that's neon purple. How does that room feel different? Which one makes you feel less stressed? Notice the colors around you: at home, at school, in stores, in restaurants. Maybe one of your favorite places to hang out happens to also be decorated in one of your favorite colors. Which colors seem to calm you or make you feel safe and snug? Choosing the colors around us can help us choose our moods, too.

A philosophical perspective: Several world religions believe that the body has seven main energy centers, called chakras, located at places like the base of the spine and the space between the eyes.

Each chakra or energy center has a corresponding color. The root chakra at the base of the spine is associated with red; the sacral chakra just below the navel is associated with orange; the solar plexus chakra just above the navel is associated with yellow; the heart chakra at the center of the chest is associated with green; the throat chakra is represented by the throat and mouth and is associated with light blue; the third eye chakra in the space between your eyebrows is associated with indigo; and the crown chakra at the top of your head is associated with purple. Many believe that if you wear light blue or meditate on the color light blue, for example, you will stimulate the throat chakra and have an easier time speaking your truth or expressing your emotions. Color or light therapy is even used as a complementary healing technique.

Make it work for you: The colors you choose for your clothing, how you decorate your living space, even how you style your hair—color can be a quick and easy way to help you shift your mood and express yourself (especially the clothes and hair part). Get familiar with your power colors! If you bring more of these colors into your environment, you will probably feel more confident, comfortable, relaxed, and happy.

The magical side of colors: Observe the fabulous, brilliant, diverse colors in nature, like the wild stripes on the San Francisco garter snake or the iridescent hues of the Nicobar pigeon. (Drop this book and go Google these color-fabulous animals now!) Sure, scientists can explain the way colors are created, but their beauty is otherworldly and their influence on how we think and feel is powerful beyond logic. Human eyes, hair, and skin come in an almost infinite variety of colors, all beautiful and unique!

The shadow side of colors: How we interpret colors can be complicated and highly personal. You might think of a black cat

What are your power colors?

Red is motivating and associated with confidence, resourcefulness, and power.

Green reminds us of nature and symbolizes good luck.

Yellow calms and brings joy—a great color for those seeking balance.

Black, like white, offers a minimalist or clean look. Black is often associated with mysticism, the arts, and high intellectual capability.

White is associated with peace, as well as clean slates, new beginnings, and winter.

Purple is royal and majestic (it was the late great pop artist Prince's favorite color) and also a signal of spiritual enlightenment.

Pink is a color of heart energy, romance, Cupid, and Valentine's Day.

Brown's earthy hue is a grounding color that gives off the feeling of gentle strength.

Blue calls to mind the sky (freedom, possibility) and emotional depth—like the blue ocean, this color suggests there's more going on below the surface.

Orange's warmth represents sunsets, summer, creativity, and playfulness (think of everyone dressing up in silly costumes on Halloween).

as mysterious, mystical, powerful, and cunning—all positive associations. Someone else might see a black cat cross their path and consider it bad luck. One person might think a white sweater is boring and bland, while someone else might think it's a relaxing break from louder or more intense colors like bright red.

Give it a try:

1. Do you have a favorite color? Wear it on a day when you need extra confidence or joy.
2. Wear a color you normally never do and notice how it moves you to behave in new ways.
3. If your bedspread is purple on top and white on the bottom, and you usually keep the purple side showing, switch it up this week.
4. Try wearing a different shade of lipstick or color of shoelaces.
5. Pay attention to the colors of the food you eat. For instance, eat a bright, colorful salad and notice if it changes your mood.
6. Observe the people around you and what colors they appear to be drawn to in their clothing, homes, and environments. Is there a connection between these colors and their moods or personalities?

Tips and tricks:

If you're feeling stuck, playing with colors is a great way to shake things up. If you always wear green (which is said to stimulate the heart chakra), try looking for orange the next time you go clothes shopping (which would stimulate your sacral chakra).

If you want to blend in and chill, choose neutral tones like tan, beige, and gray.

If you want to spice up your life, try bold patterns and bright colors.

9

Give Yourself a Break

Why it works: Judging yourself harshly creates stress. Accepting yourself as flawsome—awesome even with and sometimes because of your "flaws"—helps you form a healthier, happier relationship with yourself.

Life isn't always easy to get just right (which you already figured out for yourself at, like, age two). There's a lot expected of humans on this big ball spinning in space called earth. We all want to be talented, brave, confident, entertaining, responsible, kind, smart, and resourceful, all at the same time. But those expectations are a tall order.

Giving yourself a break means acknowledging that you won't always meet your own expectations for yourself. When you give yourself a break, you make a conscious effort not to shame yourself. It's like saying, "I had an expectation for myself about this and I didn't meet it, but it happens and I'm going to be fine." Doesn't that make your shoulders relax and your lungs let out a big sigh of relief?

A philosophical perspective: Sometimes it's much easier to be kind to or forgive other people than it is to be kind to and forgive ourselves. Philosophers might blame this on the *ego*, a necessary part of your human psyche that pushes you to be your best and achieve (all good stuff). Unfortunately your ego can be very judgmental of you. One way to neutralize your ego or keep it in check is to imagine how you would view someone else who was experiencing your same circumstances.

Make it work for you: As funny as it sounds, the more you practice giving yourself a break, the better you will perform in important situations and the better decisions you will make. That's because when you leave yourself room to be imperfect, you're taking a more relaxed attitude toward life. Stress can be very distracting and immobilizing. Lower the stakes in your life, and this calmer attitude will help you score more wins.

Examples of giving yourself a break:

1. Forgive yourself if you lose your temper with a friend, a teacher, a pet, your parents, or your boss. (Most people are pleased to accept an apology.)
2. Talk to a teacher, teammates, or band mates if a commitment you made is becoming too much to manage well. (Don't be afraid to admit that you've bitten off more than you can chew.)
3. Ask for help if you are in over your head at work or school. (This is not a sign of weakness but of good judgment.)
4. Admit to yourself or to a friend when you have let yourself down. (It's okay to be vulnerable and acknowledge that you are imperfect. This is part of how we learn and grow, and it can make other people feel comfortable admitting their own mistakes or lessons.)
5. Curl up with a pet or warm blanket for half an hour when you first get home from work or school instead of diving into homework or chores. (Transitions like this are best

done gradually—you don't have to be Captain Productive every minute of the day.)

6. Give yourself permission to blow off steam when you are in the middle of a big deadline at school or work. (Sometimes you just gotta party! Call up a friend and plan something fun and harmless like meeting for an ice cream break or a quick dance party.)

7. If you are tired or overwhelmed, put off a nonessential task until tomorrow. This isn't procrastinating—it's reevaluating your priorities and practicing good self-care.

8. Laugh at yourself! Don't take yourself so seriously. (It can feel like we are the center of the universe—in a heavy, painful way—if we never get out of our own heads. Watch a comedy to gain some perspective.)

9. Renegotiate a promise or goal. (It's normal to adjust expectations as life unfolds.)

10. Make a list of ways you are flawsome—awesome in spite of or sometimes even because of your "flaws."

The magical side of giving yourself a break: Giving yourself a break not only relieves the pressure you put on yourself, but the more you treat yourself kindly, the more others will mirror that kindness back to you. Sometimes humans will "match" the energy you meet them with. If you are angry at someone and come at them yelling and name-calling, you will probably get a similar response. Yet if you try to calmly and diplomatically explain why you are angry, you will most likely receive a more measured and productive reply.

The shadow side of giving yourself a break: Sometimes it won't be enough to give yourself a pass. If you make a big mistake or let someone down in a major way, forgive yourself for being real, and love yourself through it, but accept that there will still be consequences.

Give it a try: Find one way you can give yourself a break this week, and then notice how it feels. You can start by noticing that ego voice in your head. It's the voice that says, "You're the best!" when you ace something. But it's the same voice that says, "What were you thinking?" when you screw up. If the ego part of your mind says something judgmental to you this week, change the message by thinking a mantra like "I love myself no matter what" or "I'm getting wiser every day." Believe it or not, it's true that you are getting wiser every day!

If giving yourself a pass causes anxiety, it's probably because you aren't used to the process. If you've been really serious or hard on yourself lately you have probably made this attitude or behavior a habit. In time, it will get easier to relax, and you'll become a great judge of what you can give yourself a pass on and what you might need to take a tad more seriously.

PART 2

The Unique
Genius
of You

10

Discover Your Personal Dharma

Why it works: Once you start discovering clues to your dharma, or life purpose, which often begins to reveal itself in the teenage years or possibly even before that, you'll feel more at ease with yourself, more at home in the world, more purposeful (which increases feelings of joy and contentment), and more excited about life in general.

Why are you here? It's the most important question you can ask yourself—and there is more than one answer. Everyone has some thing or things special and distinct to offer the world. This something special that you, and only you, are meant to do can be called your path, your life purpose, or, in some Indian spiritual traditions, your *dharma*. What unique gifts do you have to offer the world? Relax, you have your whole lifetime to uncover the answers.

Part of the reason that discovering your personal dharma will take your whole lifetime is because it will change throughout your lifetime. Your dharma isn't just one thing, like your career—your dharma is your life purpose in a bigger sense. For instance, let's say your dharma is teaching. You might become an elementary school teacher, an academic, a writer, a docent, a parent, a manager, a technology trainer, a coach, or a tour guide—whatever tasks you choose to fill your life, the basis for them will be sharing ideas and knowledge with others.

Here are some common dharmas—you'll probably find that a few apply to you. And remember to move beyond stereotypes. Athletes can be very sensitive and creative, and artists can be truly tough and love sports:

Nurturer: Can include parents, spouses, and people who work with children, the elderly, and animals.

Protector: Can include people serving in the military, the government, and financial institutions as well as lawyers and those in the justice system.

Healer: Can include those who devote their lives to healing people, animals, and the planet; this healing can come about emotionally, physically, and spiritually.

Teacher: Can include teachers of all walks of life who share knowledge, whether they are kindergarten teachers or famous writers.

Rescuer: Can include firefighters, EMTs, the Coast Guard, and forest rangers.

Activist: Can include people who work for nonprofits and those who champion animals, the environment, or humans in need.

Student: Can include anyone at any age with a love for learning and the persistent desire to gain new knowledge.

Adventurer: Can include people who love travel, are bored easily, and like to change roles or homes many times to have new experiences.

Athlete: Can include people who are in touch with their bodies, crave physical challenge, and want their bodies to perform at peak levels.

Artist: Can include people with a creative bent and artists of all media, like interior decorators, dancers, writers, fashion designers, and filmmakers.

Free Spirit: Can include very independent and inspiring people who do not like to be tied down by schedules, responsibilities, or relationships. They value spontaneity and individuality.

Performer: Can include people in the public eye like actors, musicians, politicians, comedians, lecturers, commentators, and CEOs. Anyone who likes the spotlight and thrives off the energy of an audience can fit into this category.

Pioneer: Can include anyone who values doing things differently, all the rebels, people who question conventional wisdom or the status quo, risk takers, and inventors of any kind (folks who invent a new philosophy, technology, or genre of music are good examples of this archetype).

A philosophical perspective: Your dharma does not have to be specific, and it doesn't have to be a job. It might be a role you take on or a hobby you pursue. If your dharma involves working as a healer, for example, you could end up as a nurse, a doctor, a psychologist, a Reiki practitioner, an acupuncturist, a nutritionist, or an intuitive. But healers can pursue their dharma in any way imaginable, such as being a mother or working in the financial industry. Healing is needed everywhere.

Make it work for you: Many people report knowing as teens or even small children what they wanted to do with their lives. Others are much older when they blossom into their callings (yet another word for dharma). We all have many things we were "born to do," and these dharma callings will evolve over the course of our lives. Some things we are exceptional at we might choose not to pursue. It is always our free-will choice. The only thing we must do in life is try our best to be good to others and ourselves.

The magical side of discovering your personal dharma: Do you like the idea of destiny? Your favorite stories, whether they are in fantasy novels, documentaries, or your own personal life, probably deal with an element of destiny. Are there certain things you feel you are meant to do and be? When you ask yourself that question, what answers come to mind?

The shadow side of discovering your personal dharma: Don't stay in a role, situation, or relationship you have outgrown just because you believe it is part of your dharma. While you will experience challenges and setbacks in living your dharma, there should also be a certain amount of joy or sweetness in your day-to-day experience. And despite what culture might say, no one dharma is better or more worthy than another. Wanting to teach, reach, or help as many people as possible could be part of your dharma, but chasing fame for the sake of being famous can be a false or empty dharma pursuit.

Give it a try: Ask yourself the following questions. The answers are all clues to your dharma:

> What fascinates you?
> What jobs have you been drawn to since you were a young child and were first able to understand what a job was?
> What do you want to learn more about?
> What do you like to do in your spare time?
> What would you do whether you got paid or not, simply because you enjoy it so much?

What are some of your natural talents and gifts, or things that
just come easily to you?

What is most unique about your personality?

What is most unique about your life circumstances and
experiences?

What are some of the greatest challenges you have faced?

What do you often catch yourself daydreaming about being or
doing?

What type of experiences or situations have come into your life
consistently?

Tips and tricks:

Look back at famous figures in history and see if you can describe what their dharma might have been, based on their personality, job, relationships, hobbies, limitations, life challenges,
unique childhood or background, and passions.

Sometimes the events in the larger world that happen during
our lifetime are part of our dharma. Examine the dharma of
historical figures like Winston Churchill, for example, who
was the prime minister of England during World War II, or
someone in history whom you personally admire, like activist
Martin Luther King, Jr. or artist Georgia O'Keeffe, to better
help you uncover and develop your own dharma. For instance,
do you think it's possible that beyond being a statesman, fa-
ther, husband, writer, and painter, it was also part of Winston
Churchill's personal dharma to lead his country through one of
the darkest times in its history?

Imagine if someone from the future were reading about
your life in a history book. What would they say about your
dharma based on the "facts" of your life?

Remember that your dharma is unique, and will never look
exactly like another person's dharma. That is why it's called
your *personal* dharma. Kind of cool, right?

Life will present you with magical opportunities to fulfill your
dharma. Be on the lookout for them!

Your dharma should not be measured by the profit it will bring
you but by the purposefulness and fulfillment it will bring
to your life.

Dharma discovery technique:

Set this intention: "I'm working on feeling confident that I
have important contributions to offer the world, and that
my dharma will be revealed to me at the perfect points
in my life journey." Write this statement down and put it
somewhere you'll see it every day.

11

Practice Self-Love

Why it works: It's easy to love yourself when things are going your way—when you nail a performance, make the winning goal, hear your best friend say you are her favorite person in the world. And self-love is definitely about loving yourself during the good times and celebrating everything that rocks about your life.

But self-love is also about loving yourself even when you accidentally say the wrong thing and hurt someone's feelings, or get a C on the test you were expecting to ace, or lose your phone on vacation. And what about the stuff that's even bigger? Maybe you have a physical handicap that can sometimes be frustrating, or you are all thumbs at something you love and wish you could excel at, or you just moved to a new place and are having trouble making friends. When you are frustrated with yourself, your life circumstances, or something you've done, self-love is more important than ever.

Everyone makes mistakes. Everyone faces tasks or situations that are daunting. Everyone has personal traits or lifestyle conditions that make success challenging. Maybe you can't seem to master a foreign language, or you have always wished you were taller or shorter, or you have parents/guardians who are going through big financial or relationship difficulties, or you just feel different than most people and wish you had more peers you could relate to.

A philosophical perspective: Those things that we want to change about ourselves are often some of our most unique and amazing attributes, or things that will allow us to become a more compassionate, accepting person. And the mistakes we make, and the things we find challenging, often hold the biggest lessons and growth potential in our lives. So, in a sense, even the bad stuff might ultimately be all good.

Make it work for you: The real test of self-love is to be able to love yourself through some of your biggest mistakes. There are mistakes you will make in your life, that we all make, which will be traumatic and hard to sit with. Mistakes where we think, "I wish I could go back in time . . ." You might have already experienced a mistake like that, and if you have, put this book down right now and give yourself a hug. As you do, imagine everyone else who has read this book giving you a hug too, as if there are thousands of people sending you unconditional love. No matter what you did or didn't do, you deserve that love!

The magical side of self-love: You'll find that the more you are able to love yourself, the more people will naturally be attracted to you. Self-love is like a magnet that draws great people and opportunities your way. Loving yourself will also help you set better boundaries, so you won't get taken advantage of as easily. Self-love is one of the most powerful healers in the whole universe and has the ability to magically transform your life.

The shadow side of self-love: Loving yourself does not mean you are better than other people. In fact, self-love will help you appreciate others and have more empathy for them (empathy means being aware of or sensitive to the feelings or experiences of another person). Remember to stay grounded in the fact that you are a magical unicorn, but so is everyone else.

Self-love do's and don'ts:

Don't prioritize pleasing others over following your own heart.

Don't base your opinion of yourself on the opinions others have of you (this goes double for the opinions of people you don't particularly like).

Don't wait for someone else's approval to follow your dreams.

Don't concentrate on the haters.

Don't ever forget how special and important you are.

Don't punish or judge yourself when something goes wrong.

Don't ever be ashamed of who you are.

Do rest assured that if you have difficulty loving yourself or loving your life, you're not alone.

Do celebrate your victories, even the tiny ones, like when you made it to school on time after waking up late (woo-hoo!).

Do remind yourself often of what you are most proud of about yourself, either in life or a specific situation. For example, you might be really proud of how you handled a mistake or recovered from a setback.

Do spend time resting and rejuvenating.

Do notice how you treat others, which can be a reflection of how you treat yourself.

Do be as kind to yourself as you are to the people you love and value most.

Do blaze your own trail.

Do spend time with people you love.

Do invest energy in activities you love and treat yourself often.

Give it a try: Here is an exercise that's designed to jump-start the love you show yourself:

Step 1: Journal for a whole page or more on the things you love most about yourself. Add some comments about how these things make your life better, happier, easier, and healthier.

Step 2: Write down some of your recent mistakes, or biggest regrets in life. Next to each mistake or regret, write down what you learned, how you grew from this situation, or how you would handle it differently in the future. Also write down some way in which you are proud of how you handled this situation either before, during, or after.

Step 3: Make a list of your most unique traits and characteristics. When you come across something unique about you that you wish you could change, write an example of how this detail about you has made you a better or more interesting person. If you have a chronic health condition, maybe this has made you more compassionate. If one of your parents died or is somehow absent, maybe this has made you more independent and self-reliant.

You can chip away at this self-love journal exercise over the course of the next week or month—you do not have to do it all at once! Sometimes we absorb and learn more if we do things slowly.

Self-love discovery technique: Set this intention when you wake up: "Today, I will show myself more love—no matter what happens."

12

Curb the Urge to Compare & Despair

W hy it works: Comparing yourself to others, if it's done in a negative way, can open the door to self-judgment and shame. When you look at someone else's life and wish it were your own, you are focusing on *what you are not* rather than *what you are.* Comparing this way puts you in a mind-set of "lack" and "feeling not enough," as if there is something essential "missing" from your life. There are healthy ways to compare yourself to others, however, that can be inspiring and motivating.

True, someone else might have a great boyfriend or girlfriend, get As in every class, and come from a family with tons of money. But I promise that even people who seem to have everything are suffering in their own ways—often in ways you don't and may never see. Wishing you could be more like them is not taking into account the full picture of this person, which includes the struggles that you can't know or understand. Like maybe they are secretly struggling with diabetes while you have no health issues, or maybe they wish they were more creative while you are a natural-born artist, or maybe they have tons of friends but none they can really trust while you have a couple of great friends who have your back no matter what.

Everyone experiences wins and losses, joys and tragedies, and only some of them are visible to others. We notice the good in others' lives easily; we notice the negative in our own life too quickly. All that time you're spending comparing yourself to someone else is depleting you of energy you could put toward building up your own happiness and confidence.

You can't compare your life to another person's because your life was never *meant* to be just like someone else's. You will have your own graces and your own challenges: graces are gifts you are given effortlessly, like a little brother who adores you and would do anything for you, or an aptitude for math. Challenges are experiences life puts in our path to help us grow and learn and give us the chance to help others and make the world a better place. For instance, if you have a chronic illness, you might be inspired to become a doctor and help others with the same condition. If you were raised without a lot of money, you might grow up to be an investment banker who sets up charitable organizations to help the poor.

A philosophical perspective: All of your experiences, the good and the bad, shape and influence your ability to inhabit the unique life you were destined for. It's a life that will only fit you, as if you'd had your existence tailored just to your size like a suit. Now it's your job to embrace the life that's meant for you, make the most of it, and also make adjustments along the way.

Make it work for you: Sometimes when we look at another person and feel jealous, it's a sign that we would like to make a change in our lives. If you're jealous that someone else's family seems to have more vacations and nicer cars than yours, take note that you hope to have these things for yourself, and look into getting a part-time job or enrolling in a class so you can get started on a good-paying career after you finish high school. You might also look at all the ways growing up without financial abundance has developed your character, by making you less wasteful, more resourceful, and less materialistic. It's healthy to look at someone's life and say, "I'd like more of that, please!" Just remember that as you manifest whatever you'd like more of in your life—abundance, love, freedom, opportunities—those things will never look exactly the same in your life as they do in someone else's. New things you bring into your life will instead enhance and align perfectly with your own unique journey.

The magical side of not comparing yourself to others: When we don't constantly compare ourselves to others we retain our power. Instead of being interested in what is happening in other people's lives, we focus on our own. That's when we have the ability to harness the help of life to make the most of our unique journey and circumstances—and even change our circumstances for the better.

The shadow side of not comparing yourself to others: On some level, comparing yourself to others is natural and healthy. Comparing when it's done in a healthy way can be motivating, and encourage you to make positive changes in your life. If you never look around at the way other people are living you will shut yourself off to new ideas, approaches, and lifestyles.

Give it a try:

Step 1: Ask your family and friends what they admire about you! These are probably things they might occasionally be secretly jealous of.

Step 2: Write their comments in your journal.

Step 3: Now think of someone who makes you feel jealous, and write three things about them that you're jealous of.

Step 4: Next, add to that list at least one thing that you know or suspect this person struggles with.

Step 5: Now return to your list in step 3. Putting aside feelings of jealousy, ask yourself how you might bring more of those attributes to your own life.

Tips and tricks:

1. Remember that everyone has problems and challenges, whether the rest of the world can see them or not.

2. Appreciate what's unique about you and your life, and follow your individuality to discover your own brand of genius.

3. Use other people's successes as inspiration to go after your own dreams.

13

Become a Self-Awareness Samurai

Why it works: Being self-aware can help you better control your extreme emotions and reactions so you feel more energized, centered, and calm.

Have you ever found yourself observing your personality or behavior objectively? Many novels are written in the third person, with a narrator who is objective and can see into the hearts and minds of every character. Being self-aware is the practice of looking at yourself or a situation not just from your own point of view but from a higher, more detached vantage point.

When we look at situations objectively we can see other peoples' perspectives and recognize outside factors that influence a situation. When you step back from your own emotional reaction to a friend's hurtful remark, you might sense that the remark was made as an accident or because your friend was trying to get your attention and did so in an unusual and unproductive way. Getting this broader perspective on life is like when a movie camera pulls back to take in the whole scene, as opposed to a close-up of one character.

A philosophical perspective: The idea of becoming more self-aware is popular in many cultures and spiritual traditions. Modern psychology uses talk therapy to help patients become more self-aware. At its core, self-awareness is about noticing our patterns and motivations, both the ones that are positive or healthy as well as the ones that are negative or self-sabotaging. To truly change, shift, or heal a pattern, we must understand it and find out what is at its core, just like when you are getting rid of weeds in a garden. You will need to pull weeds out at the root or they will simply grow back. Sometimes at the root of a negative or self-sabotaging pattern, such as an eating disorder like anorexia or obsessive exercise, is not really the wish to be attractive or thin, but a wish to please, fit in, have more control, be perfect, punish ourselves, or receive attention, love, and help.

Make it work for you: Self-awareness is excellent at helping you identify patterns in your life that you want to change. If you observe yourself objectively, you might find that you have certain triggers that make you feel angry or out of control. If you keep ending up at an emotional place you don't like, such as stressed, hopeless, or fearful, look back on the events leading up to that familiar emotion and observe the triggers. Maybe waiting until the last moment to cram for a test is a stress trigger, concentrating on all the ways something could go wrong might be a trigger for hopelessness, and watching a violent or scary movie right before bed can be a fear trigger.

The magical side of self-awareness: Practicing self-awareness is like a prisoner getting the keys to his or her jail cell. We can vastly improve our lives and experience more happiness and peace through self-awareness. One way we do this is by being less reactive, or realizing we do not have to respond to or engage with everything that happens throughout the day, like a fish that can swim by without taking the bait.

The shadow side of self-awareness: Being too self-aware can make people overly critical of themselves. Of course, self-awareness is also never an excuse to deny your emotions: Let yourself process negative feelings like sadness or anger by crying or talking with a friend—but then move on and try to look at the situation from a more objective or detached perspective.

Give it a try: Practice being the observer or the objective narrator of your own story for one day. See how this affects your mood and attitude, and see if you can get to some of the real motivations and patterns behind why you and those around you do or say things.

Tips and tricks:

1. Develop a regular meditation practice.
2. Ask your closest friends and family members what they believe are your greatest strengths as well as your biggest areas for improvement.
3. Look for opportunities to be a diplomat or mediator when two people are in a disagreement. This will get you in the practice of seeing things from two opposing sides.
4. Pause before you take a major action step or make a significant decision and ask yourself: What is my motivation? Use your intuition to help you discover your deepest motivations. Your intuition is your powerful sixth sense that often provides you with information through feelings, dreams, ah-ha ideas, or gut instincts.
5. Avoid using stimulants like caffeine and sugar to gain more clarity. Self-awareness is about being clear, not frazzled or run-down.

6. Identify some of the main patterns in your life. Remember, some will be healthy and some will be self-sabotaging. Try to discover when these patterns started and why.

7. Notice the next time you are really angry or sad, and gain some perspective by pretending you are watching someone else experience this situation. What advice or comforting words would you offer them?

8. Become aware of when you are continually frustrated and upset around the same person or by the same situation, and ask your frustration what message it is trying to give you.

9. Observe your reactions to people and situations. If someone does something that upsets you, pause before responding or deciding what action to take. This helps you be less reactive to other people and more centered in yourself.

10. Learn your triggers, or the things that consistently make you feel extremely emotional, anxious, or out of control.

QUIZ: HOW SELF-AWARE ARE YOU?

The quizzes in this book are meant to be fun and informative. There are no right or wrong answers. No one is grading you and you do not have to share the results of a quiz with anyone. Try to resist looking ahead to the end for the answer key (that's supposed to be a surprise, and if you look ahead it will influence the way you answer the quiz). Be brave and answer honestly!

This quiz is meant to help you get an idea of how self-aware you have been lately and give you suggestions on how to become even more self-aware. Relax, take a deep breath, and enjoy!

1. How often do you take time out to meditate, journal, or walk alone in nature?

    a. Very often, like daily or several times a week. I crave these things and feel more peaceful and less stressed when they are a regular part of my routine.
    b. I almost never do these things. That's just not my style.
    c. Sometimes I do these things, when I have time or feel like I need quiet reflection.

2. When someone criticizes you, you usually:

    a. Take some time to immediately process what they said. If it feels completely off, I ignore the criticism, but if there is some truth in the comment then I take it onboard.
    b. Get pretty defensive at first. But occasionally, a few weeks or even months later, I might catch myself thinking of their comment again.

continues

Quiz: How self-aware are you?   *continued*

    Sometimes they were totally wrong, but other times I realize much later that they had a point with their criticism.

  c. Try to block it out. Honestly, if people would spend more time being sweet and less time criticizing others, the world would be a much kinder, happier place.

3. If you keep finding yourself in a certain situation you do not like—such as always being late for class or work; always feeling run-down; or always losing your temper—you usually:

  a. Get curious about why this keeps happening. Then I might talk to someone I trust and brainstorm ways to start changing or shifting this pattern so I can be happier.

  b. Try to be philosophical about it. Everyone has things in their life they don't like. I might attempt to change, but some things just are the way they are. Life is easier and simpler if you accept that.

  c. Become upset. This kind of situation reminds me that life can be unfair and cruel. I might even start to blame or judge myself for this situation.

4. When a close friend or family member is upset and acting cranky or rude, I:

  a. Try to take a step back and see what is really bothering them. It's probably not all about me forgetting to finish the laundry, but something deeper. If I can figure out what is really going on I will better know how to help.

  b. Tiptoe around them until they are feeling better.

Quiz: How self-aware are you?

    c. Ask myself, "Did I do something wrong?" Then I go out of my way to make their life easier by being very sweet, giving them a shoulder to cry on, and offering to help with their responsibilities.

5. When someone I love is really hurting, I:

    a. Do what I can to ease their suffering, offering support and encouraging them to talk about their problems. But I remind myself that it does not help to take on their pain or suffering as if it were my own. That just creates more suffering in the world. I have my own separate life and emotions.

    b. Try to distract them with something happy or funny. It takes their mind off things for a bit and keeps me from feeling down, too.

    c. Hurt with them and maybe even feel guilty if things are going well for me. When someone close to me is hurting it's very hard for me to be happy. At least my loved one knows they are not alone in their suffering.

6. When something feels off with me, I:

    a. Take a timeout to assess the problem. Am I eating too much junk food? Secretly feeling angry or stressed about something? Usually I can pinpoint the issue, and just knowing what exactly is off makes me feel so much better. I want to have the best quality life I can, and being in tune with myself helps.

    b. Shrug it off. If I can't quickly figure out what is wrong, I just push through it. Life is a roller

continues

coaster of ups and downs, and sometimes you can think too much. Not everything has a reason or an answer.

c. Feel frustrated. I don't always like to get quiet and look at what is really upsetting me, because sometimes my emotions can overwhelm me so I try not to go into the negative ones too deeply. Often I won't figure out what is off until the situation gets really bad.

7. A bully, or someone I don't know very well, tries to start a fight with me. I:

a. Stand my ground in a peaceful way. I might make a joke or roll my eyes and walk confidently away. I don't know or don't like this person, so why invest anything? Diffusing or leaving the situation is best because I try to minimize any unnecessary drama in my life. Feeding into their negative energy would probably only create more of these episodes.

b. Don't really like it, but feel I have to fight back. I mean this person started it and now I have no choice but to finish it. What else are you going to do?

c. Get very upset. I will think about the situation for days afterward, unable to get it out of my mind. But usually I am too flustered and embarrassed in the moment to know what to say or how to handle things.

Self-Awareness Samurai! (You answered mostly As):

Being self-aware might just come naturally to you. Perhaps you were a little Buddha even as a child, or maybe you have spent time developing a strong practice of self-awareness. Make it your mission to be an ambassador of self-awareness in the world. You do so just by the example you set, but you might also give people tips on self-awareness when you see they are struggling and you believe they will be open to what you have to say. It's hard to get through to people when they aren't feeling super open, so sometimes it's better not to waste your energy or create unnecessary drama by giving advice—but since you are a self-awareness pro you already knew that!

Self-Awareness Surfer (You answered mostly Bs):

You are going with the flow and surfing life's waves, my friend, and there's nothing wrong with that. It probably feels like a more chill approach. But sometimes you might accept uncomfortable situations a little too easily. You may feel like it's a hassle to look deeper into your life, your relationships, or yourself, but it's just like looking beneath the water. There is a whole beautiful, fascinating world under the surface of the ocean, one you would never guess even existed if you didn't dive deep. Remember that what is going on beneath the surface affects the outer conditions. You are not always at the mercy of life or other people. Use self-awareness to give yourself the best ride possible in this life!

Self-Awareness Sensitive (You answered mostly Cs):

Life can be scary and overwhelming, especially when you are sensitive. Being sensitive does not mean being weak, it simply means that you feel things intensely, and are very attuned to the energy and emotions of others. Another way of describing sensitivity is to say you are hyper-perceptive—you notice everything. Don't shy away from self-awareness because you are afraid of your feelings or your sensitivity. You are sensitive but also strong and powerful (sensitivity, once you learn how to work with and manage it, will become one of your greatest strengths). You have the ability to face tough situations and influence the outcome of situations toward peace and love. Set healthy emotional boundaries with others so they don't accidentally drain your energy.

PART 3

Embracing
the Magic &
Mystery
of Life

14

Find Your
Spirit Animals

Why it works: Identifying with the inspiring character traits of animals helps you tap into your own innate power. And when you feel powerful, you feel prepared to face challenges with confidence.

Certain animals are believed to have certain character traits. For example, Native American tribes believe that several animals travel with a person or family for life, acting as guides.

Have you ever noticed animals appearing out of the blue in your life? Maybe an exotic animal like an armadillo, or perhaps you keep seeing red cardinals over and over, almost as if they are in on some giant conspiracy and following you around. If an animal shows up unexpectedly, or shows up continually, it might have a message for you. Get quiet and ask your higher self (that very wise, super objective part of you) what message this animal has for you and also think about what this animal usually represents in your culture.

A philosophical perspective: Thinking about a person you admire, like a family member you look up to or a famous athlete, can make you feel inspired and positively influence your behavior and outlook. The same is true for an animal who symbolizes something to you. Unicorns, for example, are mythical animals from legend that are depicted as very rare, magical, and sought after. How are you also rare, magical, and intrinsically worthy?

Make it work for you: Sure, there are some common interpretations for many animals: butterflies are a symbol of transformation, dogs often symbolize companionship and loyalty, and owls represent wisdom. But animals can hold unique meaning for you personally, too, which has nothing to do with their cultural significance. Maybe you have a chronic health condition and the first time you were hospitalized, someone gave you a stuffed swan. Now whenever you see an image of a swan, it reminds you not only of beauty and grace (cultural meaning) but that there will always be mercy, healing, and love for you (personal meaning).

What's your spirit animal?

You don't have to see an animal in person to have it serve as your guide. Below are some common spirit animals and the traits they symbolize. You can focus on any of these animals to gain their unique strength and wisdom. Maybe a few of them have some personal meaning to you as well:

Elephant: These animals are proof that you can be both intimidating and cute! Elephants are also in danger of extinction, so if you are an elephant lover there are organizations you can join or donate to in an effort to protect them. The big, floppy ears, long trunks, and white tusks make the elephant very unique and a symbol of celebrating what is unique or special about your life. Have you ever watched

What's your spirit animal?

a baby elephant play or snuggle up to a human? If not, get on YouTube and search for a video right now! It's an example of how elephants are strong yet gentle. How can you also be strong yet gentle? Elephants are also thought to have long memories (type "elephant reunion" into You-Tube for proof—and have a tissue handy). Elephants might be a symbol of the eternal nature of your love for someone. There are people that we love forever. Send one of these people a birthday card with an elephant on the cover.

In the Indian Hindu religion, the poplar deity Ganesha is represented as having the head of an elephant.

Turtle: These four-legged reptiles can waddle around on land or paddle through the water, which makes them a great reminder to stay adaptable to your environment or current life circumstances. Has something in your life recently changed (maybe a parent remarried or a sibling moved out), calling for you to adapt? No matter where they are, turtles take their time and are known for encouraging a slower pace. If you have been busy and stressed and need to slow down, picture the turtle who won the race against the cocky hare, and pace yourself. Turtles carry their homes on their backs, so if you are traveling a lot or moving, turtles can help you remember that home is not really a place, but where the heart is.

In Japanese culture, the turtle symbolizes longevity and good luck.

Wolf: "Cunning" is one word to describe a wolf, as wolves are experts at surviving and protecting themselves. If you feel threatened because you are worried about finances or the future seems uncertain, picture a wolf and know that,

continues

What's your spirit animal? *continued*

just like this animal, you will find ways to get your needs met. You might even imagine a wolf walking beside you, or sleeping at the foot of your bed, protecting you. Or you could hang a picture of a wolf in your locker or over your desk at home. Wolves are wild animals who really don't put up with much. So, if someone is crossing your boundaries by being a taker and never a giver, or someone speaks to you disrespectfully, summon wolf energy to help you tell them, politely, to back off!

Wolves are popular in Native American culture, associated with courage and hunting. Keep in mind that "hunting" does not have to involve animals. You could be hunting for a college, volunteer job, or new friend.

Bear: The bear is considered a very grounding animal and one that reminds us of the importance of rest and solitude to rejuvenate our spirits (grizzly bears hibernate for seven months, more than half of the year). Perhaps this natural instinct to pull back from life and rest is the reason that bears are also associated with healing. Bears are fiercely protective of those they love, as anyone who has stumbled upon cubs in the woods knows. How are you protective of the people you care about?

Viking warriors wore bearskins into battle as inspiration.

Fox: Just as the wolf is thought of as cunning, the fox is believed to be clever, hence the phrase "outfox" someone. Sadly, the fox has been a popular object of prey for hunters over the ages, so these animals are also known for being quick-thinking and decisive in tough situations and for being fast and agile—traits they might have had to develop to "outfox" hunters. Perhaps a challenge in your life has made you have to develop similar traits. Is there an area of your life where you need to think outside the box or be more flexible? Call on the fox for ideas.

In many ancient cultures across the world, the fox represented trickster energy.

Rabbit: Bunnies appear nervous to humans, as they are often twitchy or fidgety. Rabbits remind us to take good care of our nervous systems by getting enough sleep, avoiding caffeine and sugar, and steering clear of unnecessary drama. (Do you really need to argue with your little brother over who should take out the trash?) Rabbits usually signal that we need to nurture ourselves more, just as your impulse when you see a fluffy bunny is to pet and soothe it.

In Aztec mythology, many divine deities are rabbits who love to party!

Nightingale: Known for their beautiful songs, nightingales sing during the day but also at night. The nightingale's nocturnal lullabies encourage us to speak our truth and express our emotions even when our lives feel dark (we've lost a loved one, had a blowup with a friend, failed an important test, found out our parents are getting divorced, have been diagnosed with a condition that sounds intimidating). The nightingale assures us the sun will come out in our lives again, but until then we need to feel safe expressing our needs and wants during challenging times. Are you afraid to tell someone in your life how you are really feeling? Ask the nightingale to give you courage and just the right words.

It's not surprising that the nightingale features in song lyrics sung by artists like Norah Jones, Trisha Yearwood, Demi Lovato, Carole King, Robyn Hitchcock, Harry Connick, Jr.,

continues

What's your spirit animal?   *continued*

Leonard Cohen, Roxy Music, Bob Dylan, Aerosmith, Tori Amos, Michael Bublé, Diana Krall, Ella Fitzgerald, Arthur Lee, Dusty Springfield, and Stevie Nicks.

Cat: Notoriously autonomous—or self-sufficient and independent—cats truly are their own masters. Cats can help us learn to take control of our lives and call our own shots. Cats are also known for being finicky. If you start seeing stray cats all the time or are constantly confronted by cat videos on social media, the message could be that you aren't being finicky or picky enough, and settling for less than you deserve or are entitled to. When you want to be your own boss, while still honoring other people's needs and truths, adopt a boss cat spirit animal!

It is believed that the Egyptians were the first to domesticate cats over three thousand years ago. Ancient Egyptian paintings portray cats lounging around homes.

Horse: If you dream about horses but don't even know how to ride one in your waking life, it might indicate that you desire more freedom—just like wild horses probably feel free when galloping across the open plains. Horses are also known to be temperamental or sensitive. Humans are also sensitive, but sometimes we don't like to admit it as some people mistakenly associate sensitivity with weakness. The horse reminds us to honor our sensitivity. Race horses, the most prized horses of all, are notoriously sensitive and also notoriously powerful, graceful, and successful. *The Horse Boy* is a thought-provoking book and documentary about a child on the autism spectrum and his unique connection to horses.

In Australia, wild horses that roam free and travel in packs are called Brumbies.

What's your spirit animal?

Tiger: This animal is very territorial, so if someone is disrespecting the earth we all inhabit by not living green, or if a bully is picking on one of your family members or friends, you might be called to defend your turf like the tiger. Just the sight of a tiger in the wild is intimidating to other animals and a reminder that you don't always have to take action to defend your turf—simply stand your ground. Seeing tigers in a movie or reading about them in books could inspire you to be more assertive in life and go after what you want, just like the tiger goes after its prey.

There are twelve animals in the Chinese zodiac, and people born in a year of the tiger are thought to be courageous, competitive, and confident. Tiger "babies" of the zodiac are believed to be action-oriented, but should watch out for acting rashly or recklessly.

Eagle: You've probably heard or read the phrase "lone eagle," and eagles represent enjoying solitary pursuits—like reading, writing, painting, inventing, gardening, working out, sinking your teeth into a juicy math problem, sewing, or cooking—just like the eagle loves to take solitary flights, unlike other birds who prefer to fly in flocks. Eagles inspire humans to gain perspective on life since they fly at such a high altitude that eagles can see an entire forest or mountain instead of just a single tree or rock. Go check out a video of an eagle in flight and see for yourself!

The bald eagle is not actually bald, but has a head covered in small white feathers. Declared an endangered species in the mid-1990s, the national bird of the United States of America is currently in no danger of extinction after concerted efforts to conserve the species.

continues

What's your spirit animal? *continued*

Sheep: Watching sheep graze on a hillside, a pastoral sight in parts of the United Kingdom like Wales, is considered a calming activity. Sheep harken back to a simpler time in history when shepherds would herd the animals and then shear them for wool (and yes, this is still how some people, maybe even your family, earn a living). Sheep also remind us of the cyclical nature of life—sheep would grow their fleece and at a certain time of year be shorn, and then the cycle would begin all over again. If your life seems hectic or out of sync with the rhythms of nature, meditate on the image of a sheep. Sheep show us that we can take from animals while not hurting them. The shepherd cares for and watches over his flock, and if the shearing is done carefully it should cause no pain to the animals. Sheep might inspire you to be kinder to animals.

The Christian ascended master Jesus is referred to as the "lamb of God" in the Bible.

Dolphin: These aquatic mammals are often described as being highly intelligent, compassionate, and remarkably friendly to humans (schools of dolphins have circled surfers and swimmers to keep them safe from shark attacks). These character traits make dolphins seem like *special* animals, which is why dolphins are a great reminder that every human is special, too. If you are feeling down on yourself, read an article about dolphins and tell yourself that you are as special as this truly stand-out species. Dolphins are incredibly playful and could even be described as the class clowns of the animal kingdom (check out a video online of dolphins being mischievous or performing by jumping up out of the water). Yet dolphins are renowned for their intellectual capability and are believed to be second only to humans in the smarts department. A dolphin's brain is four

> ## What's your spirit animal?
>
> to five times larger than it should be based on their body size, and they display levels of awareness and cognition that were once thought to be innately human. This combination of brilliance and playfulness reminds us to take a break from school and work, and have some fun. The dolphin teaches that you don't have to be serious all the time to be smart.
>
> *Poseidon, the Greek god who ruled the sea, was often associated with dolphins.*
>
> **Dog:** This animal is known for being loyal, patient, hardworking, and dependable. If you sense that the dog is one of your main spirit animals, or you adore having dogs as pets, you are probably very loyal, too. But keep in mind that you can be loyal to a fault. The dog spirit guide can teach us to be our own masters and to think for ourselves instead of just following the pack. Are there any old, outdated ideas you are still loyal to that are not really working for you? Maybe you used to enjoy playing sports, but now you are drawn to learning a musical instrument and need to reevaluate your hobbies. Dogs also remind us to follow our gut instincts. Dogs are highly intuitive animals who can often sense if a human is physically unwell or emotionally upset.
>
> *Dogs are so dependable and trustworthy that they are often used by ranchers and farmers to help herd and protect animals like cattle, chickens, and sheep.*
>
> **Flamingo:** The pink plumage of this bird is striking and gorgeous, a symbol of exotic beauty. If you want to bring more beauty into your life, get a flamingo-decorated shower curtain or put a pink flamingo in your yard. Flamingos can be great inspiration for visual artists like painters or fashion designers. Because it is gifted with fancy feathers,

continues

What's your spirit animal?   *continued*

the flamingo can encourage you to put your natural gifts on display. Are you naturally funny, or a detail person who is a born organizer? Don't be afraid to own your talents and put them to good use in the world.

In Peru, the flamingo is considered a sacred animal and is often depicted in artwork. The Andean flamingo is native to the mountains of South America.

Seal: Sometimes referred to as "dogs of the sea," seals prefer to live in large colonies. Type "seal colony" into your browser for images of seals piled on top of each other. For this reason seals are a symbol of community. If you've been feeling lonely or have been on the outs with a family member, look at images of seals hanging together to inspire you to create more intimacy in your life. The seal can encourage us to get along with others when in close quarters, like a classroom, locker room, or dorm room. Living a communal existence is about compromising and making sure everyone's needs are met.

Selkies, creatures who are part seal and part woman, are prominent in Scottish folklore and similar to the myth of the mermaid.

The magical side of working with spirit animals: Thinking about all the different kinds of animals in the world and what they symbolize might make you care more about animal rights. If you find yourself becoming an animal lover, you can give back to animals by volunteering to walk dogs at your local shelter, incorporating more vegan or vegetarian meals into your diet, or donating as a family once a month to a nonprofit that fights for the welfare of animals. Everything you need, all the traits we listed above, are already inside of you. Some, like courage, for example, may just be dormant because you've never had a situation that called this trait forth before. In that sense you are your own hero and don't really need animals or anything outside of yourself for courage. Animals are only reminders of the power and wisdom we have access to at any time.

The shadow side of working with spirit animals: Any positive character trait taken to an extreme can cause imbalances and create problems. For instance, if you are too independent, you could make life harder on yourself by never asking for help.

Give it a try: Connect with a spirit animal from the list or one that you have seen recently in nature by drawing a picture of the animal, watching a video about the animal, or reading about this animal online. Picture this spirit animal in your mind whenever you feel confused, worried, or down.

Tips and tricks:

1. You can have several spirit animals, but start with just one. If you don't know which animal to choose, let your intuition decide! Just close your eyes and let your inner wisdom conjure up an image of the animal that would be most helpful to you right now. Or think about what animal interests you most. Are you fascinated by hummingbirds? In awe of egrets? Dazzled by dragons? Or observe the animals that keep showing up in your life—either in the real world or in books and movies.

2. Once you've chosen an animal, pay attention to the way it lives and behaves. Use your head to analyze which traits will be most helpful to you and use your heart to feel the animal's energy moving inside you.

3. As time passes, surround yourself with symbols and reminders of your spirit animal. Doodle it in the margins of your notebook, make it your screen saver or social media background image, or post a photo in your locker. Each glimpse of the animal will reinforce its influence in your everyday life.

15

Get Grounded with Crystals

Why it works: Like rocks, crystals are a naturally occurring, geological solid. Unlike rocks, crystals can be translucent, or see-through, to varying degrees and are made up of highly intricate, structured lattices. Sometimes a crystal will even have other, smaller, perfectly formed "shadow" crystals inside of it that are apparent to the naked eye!

Crystals can be thousands of years old and are considered to be very grounding, perhaps because a crystal's age can ground us by reminding us of what is eternal in life—the love we have for friends and family, for example. This sense of the eternal helps put more temporary issues in perspective. When you feel grounded you feel safe, calm, and confident. Another reason crystals are grounding is because they remind us that we are connected to the earth, which can help us find our center and feel emotionally even-keeled again.

Just having pictures of nature in our homes has been shown to have a calming effect on humans, and crystals are arguably better than pictures since they are real pieces of nature. Crystals are fascinating to look at because they embody the intricacies of design that nature is capable of. And crystals come in all shapes, colors, and sizes, so you can match them to any decor! Some people believe that crystals even have healing properties.

A philosophical perspective: Crystals have long been valued by mystics, and some people believe that crystals can absorb negative energy and transform it into positive or more neutral energy. This is much like how a plant takes in carbon dioxide and transforms it into oxygen (one more reason we need to protect the rain forests). Hold a crystal and gaze at all the interesting patterns within. Like humans, crystals are complex!

Make it work for you: Crystals can improve your energy simply by making you smile and inspiring you to appreciate the unique, mysterious beauty found in nature. Some people like to keep a small crystal in their pocket or purse so that they can hold it anytime they feel stressed or scared.

Certain crystals are believed to have certain properties:

Rose Quartz: This crystal has a delightfully pale pink hue, and perhaps because of its color this crystal is said to be calming. Since rose quartz is also a crystal that represents love, you might try to find one that has been cut and polished into the shape of a heart. If you need to open your heart or work on forgiving someone else or yourself, hold rose quartz in your palm for a few minutes while you concentrate on your heart or this person.

Rose quartz makes a wonderful gift for someone you truly love.

Clear Quartz: Often translucent, clear quartz is a wonderful stone to have around if you are working on being more honest or transparent with yourself and others. This crystal, which can hide nothing, might remind you not to keep too many secrets! Use it if you want to summon the courage to speak your truth.

Keep a small piece of clear quartz near your cell-phone charger to encourage you to be authentic in your communications.

Citrine: Want to attract more abundance into your life, or just remind yourself of all the abundance you already enjoy? The sparkling yellow color of citrine is thought to be a magnet for good things. Maybe that's because this crystal resembles the color and makeup of the gold nuggets that miners searched for in the Gold Rush. The color gold often symbolizes wealth, but it also represents balance and can be a reminder that true abundance is a life where all our needs are met—not just financial but spiritual and emotional, too.

If you have been feeling out of balance, place a piece of pretty citrine, or a picture of this crystal, by your bed as a reminder to prioritize rest and relaxation.

Amethyst: If you're having trouble making a decision or seeing a situation clearly, concentrate on one of these vibrant purple crystals to help focus your mind. Amethyst is said to stimulate the third eye—a mystical concept that represents visually our ability to connect with heightened powers of perception (Hindu women sometimes wear a bindi in the middle of their forehead to represent the third eye). Your intuition, or sixth sense, something we all possess, is a power you can use to gain deeper insight into a person or situation.

Think of a situation, person, or decision that has you stumped. Then hold a piece of amethyst up to your forehead to remind you to connect with your intuition, and close your eyes. Let go of your logical mind and feel into the issue via something deeper. What thoughts or feelings do you have about this situation now?

Black tourmaline: This unique crystal is opaque (cannot be seen through). It comes in a gorgeous, rich black color and is used for protection. If you are feeling nervous about something small like an upcoming test, or something bigger like an approaching hurricane, keep a small, palm-sized piece of black tourmaline with you until the test, or the storm, passes. Anytime you are feeling anxiety, reach into your pocket or your purse and touch your crystal as you take three slow, deep breaths. Next think back on a time when you were very worried about a situation that turned out just fine.

When you are scared, hold a piece of black tourmaline, or stare at a picture of this crystal online, to anchor yourself in the idea that you are stronger and more courageous than you realize.

The magical side of crystals: Crystals are considered natural wonders for a reason—they contain mysteries of the earth. Look up images of the "crystal cave" from the BBC TV show *Merlin* and prepare to be mesmerized.

The shadow side of crystals: Crystals should be a positive influence on your life, not make you superstitious. If you don't own any crystals, you'll be fine! But if you like the look of them, or can sense their energy, start collecting crystals. In time, you might collect a whole crystal garden that can live in your bedroom! Crystals don't have to be expensive to work and can be found very affordably priced. Whenever you go on vacation, you might look for shops that sell affordable crystals.

Give it a try: Find a shop or museum in your town that sells or displays crystals and take a walk through, examining all the different varieties. If you cannot find a shop or museum to view crystals, look at images of different types of crystals online. How do you feel after looking at a crystal, either in your hand or in a photo? What kind would you choose to own?

16

Wish on a Star

Why it works: What do you wish for most? What is closest to your heart? What do you want to see change in your own life? What do you want to see change in the world? There is great value in making a wish, or sending out a request from your heart, like a beacon of light into the universe. Wishing, or expressing your deepest desires, helps you get clear about what you want and what is important to you.

Making a wish gets you in touch with hope. Flour is the basic ingredient for making a cake, and hope is the basic ingredient for making a dream come true. Even if we don't get exactly what we hope for, hope gets us closer to our dreams. Wishing is an expression of hope. If you have felt hopeless lately, wish for something, even something very small, and see if hope does not begin to grow inside you again.

A philosophical perspective: Many spiritual traditions believe that asking life for something specific in a direct manner—whether you wish in your thoughts, your journal, during prayer, while meditating, or as you express your feelings to a friend—brings you closer to what you desire or even helps draw it to you.

Make it work for you: Sometimes a miracle happens and what you desire falls effortlessly into your life. But usually wishing is not enough to make something come true. Along with identifying and focusing on what you want by wishing for it and asking life to help you out, you will likely need to take action steps to make this wish come true. If you wish you had more money, you might need to get a side job or offer to do more babysitting. If you wish for more friends, you might have to join a club or participate in new activities that will bring you into contact with new people with similar interests. But just sending out that magical wish from your heart can help draw ideal people and opportunities to you, like little gifts from life.

Wishes you might send out into the universe:

I wish for a friend who really understands and appreciates me.

I wish that the person who picks on me will have a change of heart.

I wish for a way to showcase my talents.

I wish to feel healthier and stronger.

I wish to get a second chance.

I wish to give the best performance I have in me at the concert/ game tonight.

I wish my family can learn to get along despite our differences.

I wish to do something with my life that makes the world a better place.

I wish to learn how to cope with my anxiety so I feel more peaceful and free.

I wish to feel protected and safe.

I wish to feel special and loved.

I wish to treat others as I would like to be treated.

I wish to be better at surrendering to circumstances that are out of my control.

I wish that instead of settling, I can have the patience to wait for something better to come along.

I wish for inspiration to start an exciting new hobby.

I wish to find a lot of reasons to smile today.

I wish to discover a fascinating subject that I will want to learn more about.

I wish something fun and unexpected happens to me today.

I wish my sibling will accept my apology.

I wish to find healthy ways to blow off steam this week.

I wish to find a way to go to college or trade school.

I wish to get a job that's meaningful and fulfilling.

I wish to be more productive today.

I wish I didn't feel so alone.

I wish my friend/family member would get help for their addiction.

I wish that violence in my country or in my neighborhood would stop.

I wish the world would become a more peaceful and loving place.

The magical side of wishing: The magic of wish making is the hope it brings. As you blow out the candles on a birthday cake, find a four-leaf clover, throw a penny into a fountain, see a shooting star, or catch a glimpse of a rainbow, make a wish. You are allowing yourself to think beyond everyday limitations and hope for something bigger or better.

The shadow side of wishing: As we all know, wishes don't always come true—even if the wish is very important or dear to our hearts. Don't let that stop you from wishing, though, and remembering that no matter the outcome there is magic in making a wish. It's one way your heart expresses itself. If you make a wish and it doesn't come true, think back to a time when you wished for something and it came true beyond your wildest imagination. Use that experience to inspire you to keep wishing!

Give it a try: You can wish anytime you want: in the halls between classes, as you're sitting in a movie theater, before a big test, after you try out a new trick on your skateboard. But it can be fun to making wishing a little ritual: light a candle as you whisper your wish, or write your wish on a piece of paper and then sleep with it under your pillow every night for a week.

Exercise for wishing on a star:

Step 1: Go outside on a clear night.

Step 2: Find the brightest star in the sky.

Step 3: See if the light from this star awakens anything in you. Does it make you think of a wish you long for that hasn't come true yet, or maybe this star reminds you of something you are afraid to wish for?

Step 4: The night sky reminds us of magic and possibilities, which makes this an ideal time to make a wish, as if our wishes are so powerful that they can stretch all the way up to the stars. While watching your star glow, make a wish.

Step 5: Write the wish in your journal. Also write down one action step you could take right now, big or small, that would help make this wish come true.

Step 6: Watch for signs in the coming weeks that your wish was magically heard by the universe, and that life might be trying to help your wish come true. Or you might start to see evidence of an even more appropriate wish, something different you hadn't thought of, coming true.

17

Spot the Signs from Life

Why it works: You might send life a message by wishing on a star, but have you ever wondered if life can send you a message back? All of our collective energy—people, plants, animals—makes up its own giant energy, which we are both a part of and separate from. You can tap into this universal energy for wisdom and knowledge.

Signs are all around us, but we might miss them if we're not paying attention. If you're struggling with something in your life, stay alert to what is going on around you. A friend might offer some very wise advice that helps you make sense of your situation. Or you might see a display of books at the store that calls to you, and as you thumb through them you realize one of the books has a section on exactly what you're going through.

A philosophical perspective: These hints from life are always helpful and meant to gently point you in the right direction, bring new opportunities into your life, or ease your suffering. You might think of these signs as happy accidents or feel they have deep spiritual meaning and are answers to your prayers. You get to decide what the events of your life mean to you, and everyone will have a slightly different take on this interesting journey we call the human existence.

Make it work for you: If you are struggling with a problem, look around for signs or hidden meaning. Think of yourself as a detective looking for clues to your own life. Your life is the most important case you will ever be assigned!

Examples of common signs from life:

Synchronicities: Scholar and psychologist Carl Jung defined synchronicities as "meaningful coincidences." Perhaps you are feeling down, and out of the blue a friend who lives in another part of the country calls you and asks, "What's up?" You have a long heart-to-heart and feel so much better afterward. You never would have thought to call this friend and talk about your feelings, but this synchronicity of your friend calling unexpectedly when you were down gave you the perfect opportunity to talk through your emotions and situation.

Words of other people: Wisdom doesn't have to come from people we know and love, or even people we like! Maybe someone you normally find annoying says something really insightful that applies to what you're going through. Perhaps this person is not so annoying after all! Words of wisdom that are comforting, inspiring, or enlightening can come from people we interact with every day, whether

continues

they are close friends or complete strangers in line next to us at the grocery store.

Music: Did you ever walk into a store and hear one of your favorite songs playing? If you're feeling lonely or sad, randomly hearing music you love can make you feel better instantly. Maybe you always have a song that pumps you up and this song comes on the radio as you are driving to a big debate match. Suddenly the butterflies in your stomach settle and you begin to feel confident!

Nature: Being outside in nature is the perfect place to hunt for signs. You might encounter a rabbit or a fox on a hike and feel like this animal has a message for you (check out some meanings for rabbits and foxes in the Find Your Spirit Animal section of this book). Noticing that the wind blowing leaves off the trees during a walk might be a sign, making you suddenly realize it's time for you to start letting go of some things in your life. Catching a sunrise could inspire you to make a new beginning in a relationship, at work, or in school.

Opportunities: Have you ever been given an opportunity out of the blue? Like your friend's family offering to take you on a free trip somewhere, or a relative offering to teach you to play the drums, or a neighbor offering to let you mow their very small lawn for a nice price? Maybe you got the opportunity to help someone in desperate need. Life loves to send us opportunities to learn, grow, have fun, and give back.

The magical side of signs: When you recognize a signal from life, you realize the universe cares for you enough to send you messages. We are all important and loved!

The shadow side of signs: Sometimes it can be difficult to know the meaning of a sign. And sometimes signs don't have deeper messages or meanings at all—they are simply there to remind you that you are not alone. If you aren't sure what to think about a sign you've noticed, try talking about it with a friend or writing about it in your journal.

Give it a try: The best way to get more signs from life is to simply be awake to the present moment. Pay more attention to your life as it happens in real time, as opposed to worrying about the future or regretting the past. Life sends us signs constantly, but we might miss them if we are rushing around or stuck in our own heads. Observe what is going on around you, especially patterns or things that reoccur, and really listen when people talk. Listen not just with your ears but with your feelings and intuition.

Exercise for increasing and recognizing signs from life:

Step 1. Ask for a sign about something you're struggling with or find confusing. You can ask for this sign in your thoughts, journal, or during meditation. (Try not to ask for anything too specific, like "I want to see a white feather tomorrow at noon if my crush likes me back." Instead ask, "I'd like a sign to help me figure out how my crush feels about me" or "I'd like a sign to give me the courage to tell my crush how I feel about them.")

Step 2. Stay alert and on the lookout for a sign about this issue. Be relaxed and go about your life in a normal fashion, but remember that signs can come anywhere and at anytime. Watching for signs should not cause anxiety, but it can make you be more present during your daily life, which is a good thing!

Step 3. After you receive the sign, record it in your journal. You might also jot down any initial ideas regarding what the sign meant. Sometimes our first impressions hold valuable information.

Step 4. Give yourself a few more days to think about the meaning of this sign. You will probably discover there is more than one meaning or interpretation that is helpful or informative.

Tips and tricks:

1. A sign could be anything—a baby's smile or a sprinkled donut. If it stands out to you as meaningful, it's a sign.
2. A sign is often accompanied by an "ah-ha" feeling.
3. When you look back on your day in the evening, the signs are the memories that stand out.
4. You and a friend may experience the exact same thing (like a line from a movie, or an interaction with a stranger at a store), but it holds no special or deeper meaning for your friend. Signs are usually tailor-made to resonate just with you, so don't be surprised or disappointed if what feels like a sign to you was "no big deal" to someone else.

18

Explore Aromatherapy

Why it works: Aromatherapy is the practice of using scents to calm or invigorate—and even heal. Smelling things you like—such as an apple pie baking in the oven or a vase full of fresh flowers on your kitchen table—makes you happier, and joy is an antidote to stress.

Smell might be one of the five senses you think about the least. But your sense of smell is powerful, and can have a powerful effect on your mood. Think about how you feel when you're smelling fresh clean laundry (maybe you use a natural sweet-smelling lavender detergent). Now think about a not-so-appetizing smell, like when someone forgot to take out the kitty litter. (Okay—now stop thinking of that. It's too gross.)

Some things are universally considered good or bad smelling, but others are more subjective (or up to individual taste). You might love the smell of fresh-cut grass in the summer, but if your sibling has allergies they will have a very different take on this smell! Either way, smells conjure related feelings within us, and when you know how smells make you feel, you can put them to good use when you're feeling stressed or down.

A philosophical perspective: Some people feel that scents can actually clear the energy of a room. Energy is something you cannot see or touch, but can feel. When you walk into a room after there has been a big fight or after a big celebration, you might feel different types of energy. Spiritual spaces usually have strong, calming energy, and many religions and cultures across the world use incense to cleanse and purify holy spaces. Energy can become stagnant, and aromatherapy is thought to transform that energy by uplifting the vibes.

Make it work for you: Aromatherapy comes in many forms: pure essential oils that you buy in a small vial, room sprays, body sprays, and incense. You can also buy diffusers that emit a steady, small stream of mist or vapor into the air, filled with essential oil. Choose aromatherapy products that use natural ingredients: This is better for the environment and will protect you if you are sensitive to chemicals in the air or on your skin. You can buy aromatherapy sprays in regular stores and pharmacies; many brands are affordable and you can try a variety of scents to discover which work best for you.

Common aromatherapy fragrances:

Jasmine: The delicate flowers of this plant are known for balancing mood and emotions, whether you are feeling a little blue or a bit anxious. Jasmine is a popular addition to small herb gardens that can be grown indoors or on a windowsill. Check out pics of herb gardens online for inspiration!

Go to your local plant store and breathe in some jasmine, or buy a small plant to take home with you.

Lavender: This sweet-smelling purple plant is thought to have a calming influence. Lavender is great if you've had a long day and want to de-stress with some aromatherapy. You can hit the local farmers' market for fresh dried lavender that will not only smell great for weeks, but look pretty displayed in a mason jar, pitcher, or whatever you use to hold flowers.

Get some aromatherapy lavender-scented bath salts (find a natural one with no extra chemicals, dyes, or perfumes) and hop in the tub!

Citrus: An energizing scent—think of digging into half a grapefruit or enjoying a glass of fresh lemon water when you think of this uplifting smell. In the morning, we are looking for something to get us going and bring our energy up to meet the day, and citrus aromatherapy is meant to do just that.

Find a citrus body spray and spritz yourself down when you get out of the shower, put your nose into a bowl of tangerine-scented potpourri, or lather down with some lemon verbena lotion to get your morning energy flowing!

Vanilla: Rich, musky vanilla almost has a masculine feel and is a main ingredient in many perfumes and colognes. So, vanilla might be one to try when you are feeling romantic or want to feel attractive. It's also associated with happiness, so if you want to look on the bright side, get some vanilla-scented potpourri and keep it in a pretty bowl in your room.

Save up for an aromatherapy diffuser and then fill your room with the scent of vanilla while you get ready for a date or a group outing where you will see your crush.

Peppermint/eucalyptus: Mentioning these two together makes sense as they both have strong, bracing smells that are associated with healing and cleansing. If you had a bad fight with one of your besties over the phone while sitting in your room, you can spray some eucalyptus aromatherapy into each corner of the room to cleanse the vibes and remind yourself why this person became a best friend in the first place.

If you're feeling ill with a cold or tummy ache, make yourself a nice cup of peppermint tea, but take a minute to inhale that healing peppermint aroma before you even have the first sip.

Sage: This powerful herb is often used by Native Americans to cleanse and purify, and it is still popular to buy a big "sage stick" to clear the energy of a space. Energy clearing of this kind can be done on a regular basis. After you give a home or apartment or room a good physical clean, it can be fun to give the space an energetic clean by simply lighting a small, wrapped bundle of sage or lighting a sage-scented incense stick. Slowly and thoughtfully, wave the sage around the room. As you watch the trails of smoke dance in the air, think of things you want to release from or bring into this space. (Remember that when you are working with fire, like lighting a candle, incense, or herbs, you should do so in a safe place and make sure that the fire goes out completely before walking away. Burning candles and incense should never be left unattended.)

Sage is also associated with spirituality, so the next time you pray or meditate, light a little sage to increase your spiritual connection.

Pine: Have you ever taken a walk in a dense forest? There are some amazing smells going on: tree bark, sap, wet leaves, mud, wildflowers . . . and if you are lucky, pine. Pine aromatherapy is popular with nature lovers, so if you're the type who would ALWAYS rather be outdoors, get some pine aromatherapy for your car and hang it from your rear-view mirror.

Pine-scented candles could scratch your itch if you're yearning to get outdoors but are temporarily stuck inside.

Rose: This flower is associated with the heart, and rose is a scent you can turn to for inspiration to heal heartbreak. Whether you are grieving the loss of a pet or a family member who passed on, a friend who moved away or just moved away from you, a romantic breakup, or a disappointment at work or school when you had your heart set on something that did not work out, burn a rose-scented candle or incense stick and sit down with your journal. Pour your heart out about your feelings. Writing can be a very therapeutic way to process your emotions.

Wear rose-scented body sprays or perfumes when you need encouragement to do something nice for yourself—like ask someone for a hug or curl up with your favorite movie.

The magical side of aromatherapy: It's amazing that something as basic as a scent can affect your mood, and there are so many scents to play with! In general, aromatherapy is a very affordable hobby.

The shadow side of aromatherapy: Just as some scents lift our spirits, others can bring us down, so choose your aromas carefully. Also, if you have very sensitive skin, be careful when applying aromatherapy to your body. When spraying aromatherapy near clothing or sheets, test it first to make sure it will not leave a stain on the fabric.

Give it a try: Pick out an essential oil or spray and put some on your wrists or spray some in your room each morning for one week. See if this affects your mood.

Tips and tricks:

1. After a good cry in your bedroom, spray some aromatherapy to reinforce a fresh, new beginning.
2. Before bed, lightly spray your sheets with your favorite scent to bring the aroma's benefits into your dreams.
3. If you have trouble sleeping, release a calming aromatherapy scent, like lavender, through a diffuser. It's like a "smell lullaby"!
4. Before a big day at school or work, spray some citrus aromatherapy to invigorate your energy.
5. If you are feeling sad or stressed, light an aromatherapy candle and take some deep breaths in and out as you watch the flame flicker. The combination of scent and light can calm and ground you.

19

Make Your Own Full Moon Rituals

Why it works: Humans have always been fascinated by the moon and its cycles. Ancient cultures of India, China, Africa, Europe, and the Americas believed the moon affected plant, animal, and human life on earth. The full moon certainly affects the tides (take a walk by a river or ocean on the day of or day before a full moon and you'll see for yourself), and some like to say that the full moon affects human emotions (which is where the term "lunatic" comes from). No one can deny that the full moon brightens up the night with its disarming glow.

In modern times, many cultures have moved away from rituals. Before the Industrial Revolution many people worked the land and relied on it exclusively not just for food but for all their survival needs. Therefore, people once had a more intimate relationship with the earth and the cycles of nature. A regular natural phenomenon like a big, gorgeous full moon every month was an excuse to celebrate, give thanks, or perform ceremonies. Many people today see the full moon's luminosity as an invitation to shine some light on issues in their own lives.

A philosophical perspective: The full moon can be a great time to check in with yourself to process your emotions, face your fears, touch base with your intuition for guidance, and reevaluate your goals. What in your life are you afraid to look at? Maybe you're getting ready to graduate high school and you're nervous about the future or feeling like you don't have a plan. Relax, you are super young and there is plenty of time to get a plan together. But the full moon might be a good time to examine your options—get a job, go to trade school, enroll in college, volunteer, or travel. You might also use the full moon to reflect on what has changed for you in the past month leading up to the full moon. Sometimes life happens very fast, and changes at home, with friends, or even in ourselves get swept under the rug in the hustle and bustle of modern life.

Make it work for you: It's more imperative than ever that all of humanity, all over the planet, join together to conserve the earth and its resources. You don't have to perform a full moon ritual every month, although you can. The point is that engaging in a nature-based ritual will make you mindful of the living earth beneath your feet, and make you more apt to recycle, eat organic, and become a conscious consumer. Being a conscious consumer means that when you buy something, you think of where it came from, what it's made of, how it's packaged, and how your purchase will affect the planet and the people who made the product.

You might have heard full moons referred to by unique names in weather reports. The following list will enable you to impress your friends by throwing "wolf moon" casually into conversation next January! According to *National Geographic* magazine, "ancient cultures the world over have given these full moons names based on the behavior of the plants, animals, or weather during that month."

January's Wolf Moon: This moon got its name because back in the day, people often went hungry in winter because provisions like grain stores ran low before the spring harvest came to replenish them. Hungry dogs howled for food (if you recall from the Find Your Spirit Animal section, wolves represent survival needs). There are people starving right now all over the world—probably not far from where you live.

Go online during January's full moon and make a donation to an organization committed to ending world hunger or make a food donation to a local charity.

February's Snow Moon: In North America, it's typically colder in February so you might see the full moon rise above bare, white branches. In Australia, where the seasons are flipped compared to places like the United States, February is part of the summer and can be very hot and muggy. Down Under you might call this the summer moon.

Winter is a natural time to retreat and reflect. Use February's snow moon as an excuse to stay inside and journal about your fears and hopes.

March's Worm Moon: Native Americans named this moon because when the earth begins to thaw from winter's deep freeze, fat earthworms come up from the muddy ground. Spring is a time for new beginnings (think of baby animals being born and little kids getting out of school for the summer).

During March's full moon, concentrate on what new things you want to bring into your life.

April's Pink Moon: So named because of a pink flower called wild ground phlox, which blooms in springtime and grows in North America. In other cultures this moon is called the sprouting grass moon, the egg moon, and the fish moon. Although the moon might sometimes appear to have a pinkish hue, the planet itself never changes color—but how cool would it be if it did!

During April's full moon, think about what in your life sometimes appears to change but never actually does. Your love for family and friends might be a good example since even though you love them, they sometimes drive you crazy. Or maybe your commitment to a cause like animal rights, or your commitment to becoming a better writer or artist, appears to wax and wane as you have time to devote to it, but it's always near and dear to your heart.

May's Flower Moon: Flowers offer a fleeting beauty that is on full display this month. Visit a botanical garden or park near you or take a hike in nature to get the full benefit of May's flowers. You can always pick up fresh flowers and put them somewhere you'll notice the blooms every day. Sometimes you have to stop and take advantage of the present moment to enjoy things that are fleeting.

On the day of May's full moon, make a list of things you don't want to miss. If you're graduating school, maybe it's one last lunch with your friends. Or maybe you don't want to miss holding a baby sibling or cousin before they get big enough to crawl and run away from you!

June's Strawberry Moon: The strawberry moon often sits low in the northern hemisphere, allowing the earth's atmosphere to give it a warm tint. In Europe, this is known as the rose moon, and sometimes it is referred to as the honey moon because so many people get married in June. What do all three of these—strawberries, roses, and honey—have in common? They are almost universally considered pleasurable. This full moon could inspire you to focus on what is pleasurable in your life.

Let June's full moon nudge you to set the intention to have more fun, blow off steam, follow your passion, or pay more attention to life's simple pleasures—stuff like roses, honey, and strawberries!

July's Buck Moon: Male deer shed their antlers and in July regrow them, which is how this full moon was named. Shedding the old to focus on the new is one of the most basic cycles of nature. What have you outgrown in your life? Has something already come along to replace it? Maybe a hobby you used to love is now a little boring, or maybe you find yourself wanting to spend a lot of time with a brand-new friend.

July's full moon might have you thinking of what you need to let go of, or what no longer serves your happiness or growth, and what shiny, interesting new things you want to explore instead.

August's Sturgeon or Red Moon: Native American fishing tribes named the full moon after sturgeons because in August the fish were plentiful. It is also known as the Red Moon because August in North America is often full of long, hot summer days where the sun stays out late, and the moon often looks red through the humid haze. But back to those fish. August could be a great month to practice gratitude, just like native peoples did when the fish were plentiful.

On the day of August's full moon, ask yourself, "What do I have an abundance of?" Maybe it's love, friends, talent, opportunities, downtime, health, patience, courage, support. Give thanks for your abundance—this will help you notice more blessings in your life and maybe even draw more abundance to you.

September's Harvest Moon: Fall, or following the Autumn Equinox, is a time to harvest crops, which might make you think about your own harvest. Sometimes things happen in our lives—both positive and negative—that were completely unplanned and out of our control. But other times the seeds we plant become the harvest we reap.

You might use September's full moon as an excuse to plant some new seeds in your life so that this time next year you can enjoy the harvest, like getting on a health kick or starting to learn a new language. Also look back on the seeds you planted in the past that have now come to harvest—some of this harvest you might like and other parts of it you might regret. Use the positive as inspiration and the negative as a lesson or hard-won wisdom.

October's Hunter or Blood Moon: Native Americans hunt in October to be able to store enough food to last through the winter, when hunting is not so easy or plentiful. October could make you wonder what you have in reserve. Are you getting enough rest so that you have the reserves to study, work, and play hard? If you have a job or an allowance, have you started a savings account? Any bank will be thrilled to have a representative sit down and help you open one.

Since the October full moon represents hunting, this month ask yourself what you are on the hunt for. Maybe it's better grades, help with your OCD, an inspiring career, a cool volunteer job, an adult you can trust and rely on, or a new circle of friends.

November's Beaver Moon: Beavers are known as builders, constructing dams, canals, and lodges out of natural materials—with the help of their strong teeth. (Perfect excuse for a YouTube break to watch some furry animals at work. Watching someone else be productive counts as being productive, right?) There are many things that humans build: homes, relationships, careers, health, financial security, self-esteem. You're probably in the process of building something in your life right now. Humans always are.

November's full moon could be a good time to take stock of where you are in a project or goal, just like the manager of a construction site will periodically stop, step back, consult the plans, and see how the building of a home or office complex is progressing.

December's Cold Moon or Long Night Moon: Winter, whether you're in the northern or southern hemisphere, means long nights and less sun. Instead of being bummed that you are sometimes stuck indoors, use winter as a wonderful time to do inner work. What would you like to change or improve about your life? Winter is a great chance to explore this question. It's also an ideal time to catch up with family and friends and have deep talks.

Indulge in a long, cozy chat with someone you love or admire near December's full moon. Notice what kind of insights or emotions this talk inspires.

The magical side of full moon energy: Thinking about the moon makes you realize how small the earth is when you consider the entire galaxy. Do a little research on the stars by checking out a library book on the subject or watching a documentary on space. Don't you wonder what else is out there?

The shadow side of full moon energy: You don't need the full moon to set an intention or make a change in your life . . . or even to ask for help from the universe. The benefit of full moons is largely symbolic (but symbols are powerful tools and motivators). And the full moon isn't the only time you might perform a moon-based ritual. The new moon, when the moon is dark in the night sky, is a popular time to set new intentions.

Give it a try: Pick a month and perform your own full moon ceremony. Improvise to include any elements of ritual you want, like candles, incense, chanting, soft music, or meditation. You can also simply stand outside underneath the glow of the full moon and set the intention for light to be shed on something you're struggling with. Then notice any ah-ha thoughts you have or synchronicities you experience in the coming days.

Full moon ceremony tips:

1. A full moon ceremony might involve you setting an intention, asking a question of the universe, making a wish, reflecting on your life, or writing in your journal.
2. You don't have to do this outside, although if you have a cool porch—go for it!
3. If you do your ceremony inside, step outside or look out a window to spend a few minutes meditating on the luminous full moon and its magical, potent energy!
4. Lighting a candle at the beginning, and blowing it out at the end, are great ways to symbolically open and close a ritual. Or you can ring a bell or strike a singing bowl at the beginning and end of your ritual.

20

Know the Difference Between Giving Up & Surrendering

Why it works: There are times in life when you need to take a step back from a relationship, a dream, a goal, a situation, or a project. After you've done everything you can think of to make something work, it's time to surrender. Surrender, not give up! Giving up is when you walk away and close the door completely. Surrendering is when you walk away but leave the door open.

If you've been plugging away at a goal or a project and it's not coming together like you wanted, it can be very relaxing to walk away for a little while. You might be struggling with a math exercise and step away for a twenty-minute nap or chill-out break. Or you might have been trying out for a sports team and when you don't make the cut have to walk away for a whole year before you can try out again next season. Surrendering is coming back to the math problem after a nap or being open to trying out again for the sports team next year if you still feel like it then. Giving up would be throwing your math homework in the trash and playing a video game all night instead, or vowing you will never play that organized sport again in your whole life.

When you surrender, you allow a situation or relationship some space and breathing room to evolve, or just allow yourself a chance to look at things with fresh eyes when you come back.

A philosophical perspective: Surrendering is an act of faith, a way of trusting that life will bring you to the people and situations most suited to your happiness, growth, and healing. When you stop rowing, put up the oars, and let the river of life take you, you sometimes get closer to your dreams than if you are striving. Or surrendering one dream might lead you to discovering a more appropriate dream. As the saying goes, when one door shuts, another door opens. Often the doors that shut are ones we were never meant to walk through in the first place.

Make it work for you: Sometimes you really need to give up. If your crush doesn't like you back, it's probably healthier to give up and move on to someone who will return your feelings. If you aren't excelling at a sport, or even enjoying it, giving up could make room for you to find other interests that are better suited to your talents and sensibilities. If you aren't sure whether you should surrender or give up, first surrender. That space will help you decide if the distance you've created should be temporary or permanent.

The magical side of surrendering: When we feel passionately about something—a person, a dream, a goal—letting it go by giving up can be painful. Surrendering is an act of self-care and self-love because it offers you a gentler way to move on.

The shadow side of surrendering: Surrendering isn't always helpful or appropriate. For instance, when you're preparing for

Why surrender?

Surrender feels peaceful and is often accompanied by a sense of **relief**.

Surrender feels moderate or **balanced**, as opposed to extreme or intense.

Surrender is an intellectual decision made over time after **careful consideration**, as opposed to a strong emotional reaction in the heat of the moment.

Surrendering is stepping to the side so time, space, and life itself can work magic and **miracles**.

Surrender is acknowledging that you have **limited control** over a person or situation, as opposed to making a self-sabotaging action simply to feel in control.

Surrender encourages change and **growth**.

Surrender helps you see things from **new perspectives** or angles.

Surrender is admitting that you might not have all the answers and there could be **another way**.

Surrender is being **open** as opposed to closed off or shut down.

Surrender is relaxing and **soothing** as opposed to dramatic and exhausting.

Surrender invites life to bring **grace**, new people, and new opportunities to you.

Surrender involves continuing to take appropriate **action steps**, as opposed to throwing up your hands.

Surrender is being **flexible with the timing** of a situation, as opposed to saying, "now or never."

a test or facing an illness, you can't afford to sit back and wait to see what happens: you have to study, or take medicine, and right away. Later, once the test is behind you or you've recovered from your illness/injury, you can process the experience in your own time.

Give it a try: Identify a situation in your life you could surrender to for more peace and clarity. What would surrendering look like? Letting go of a friendship? Moving on to a new project? Putting off making a decision to let a situation evolve?

Try sharing your intentions for surrendering with a friend. Having a surrender buddy can encourage you both to practice your surrendering skills. Over time, the more you engage with the energy of surrendering, the more natural it will feel.

PART 4

Rock-Star
Rituals

21

Tap into Your Warrior Energy

Why it works: Warrior energy gets you in touch with the hero inside, which can make you feel stronger and more confident.

What do you picture when you read the word "warrior"? Maybe it's your favorite X-Man (or woman). You might picture a famous feminist like Susan B. Anthony, or an animal rights activist like Jane Goodall, or a badass performer with a message about the way we live, like Beyoncé. Whether warriors have muscles and use their bodies to fight their battles or are brilliant and use their minds or are compassionate and use their hearts, all warriors have one thing in common: uncommon strength and resiliency.

Did you know that all people have natural warrior energy? Some of us are in touch with it and others aren't as much. You might have gotten in touch with your warrior energy when a friend was bullied and you stood up for them, or maybe you got sick or injured and had to fight your way back to health. Whenever you need to become the hero of your own story, you can summon your own warrior energy.

Some people have a little more warrior in them than others. These are the folks who might be attracted to working in an

emergency room, fighting fires, signing up for the military, training to be professional athletes, touring the world as rock musicians, working for a nonprofit, devoting their lives to activism,
putting everything into their art or small business, raising a family
as a single parent, or fostering special-needs children. Any road
that is rewarding yet challenging is the path of a true warrior.

A philosophical perspective: What qualities do you feel make
up a warrior? One essential quality of a warrior is having a code of
honor, or fighting for what the warrior believes to be right, noble,
worthy, or necessary. Think of someone you truly admire and respect. Chances are they possess a strong, natural warrior energy!

Make it work for you: Think back on a time when you had to
summon your inner warrior. Maybe you had to find the courage
to start a new school where you knew no one. Perhaps you spoke
your mind when you were in a group of people you knew would
disagree with you, or stood up for a cause that wasn't popular but
was close to your heart. Probably you've needed to dig deep to find
the strength to stick out a project or class or job or chore that you
desperately wanted to walk away from. Every day we are given
opportunities to tap into our natural warrior energy.

The magical side of warrior energy: When you tap into warrior
energy, you realize you are capable of more than you imagined.
You are always stronger and more resilient than you know!

The shadow side of warrior energy: Warriors are great at powering through difficult situations—some people almost thrive in
this environment! But that's not always the best path forward.
There is an old saying that a warrior knows when to draw their
sword and when to sheath it (or put it away). Check in with your

intuition to decide if warrior energy is the best way to handle a situation. If you're run-down, exhausted, cranky, or everyone and everything is getting on your nerves, it's probably a sign you need a break, need to reevaluate your approach to a situation, or need to ask for more help and support. This would be tapping into your nurturing energy. People with strong warrior energy often have a tendency to try and go it alone—remember that it's okay and even important to get help and support.

Warrior Energy Do's and Don'ts:

Do take healthy risks.

Do push yourself past your known boundaries.

Do defend nature and animals—they can't always defend themselves and need your help.

Do stand up for those who are vulnerable or less fortunate than you.

Do encourage people to live green and be conscious consumers.

Do ask for help and support when you need it.

Do expect grace and miracles to assist you—you don't have to do it all alone!

Do be flexible and open to change and other points of view.

Do follow your own path and stay true to yourself.

Don't do something that will put your physical health or the physical health of someone else in danger.

Don't make someone look small so you can appear big.

Don't take advantage of someone's naiveté or kindness.

Don't make life harder on yourself than it has to be just to prove how strong you are.

Don't push yourself so far past your limits that you get sick, stressed, or run-down.

Don't compromise on your principles.
Don't settle a fight with your fists.
Don't take the easy way out.

Give it a try:

Step 1. Create an image of the ultimate warrior in your journal, either by drawing, collage art, or printing out a picture of a real person or fictional character from the web.

Step 2. Next to the image, write ten sentences about why this image represents an admirable warrior.

Step 3. How can you adopt more of these character traits in your own life?

QUIZ: WHAT TYPE OF WARRIOR ARE YOU?

We all have an inner warrior, a way we like to take on a challenge, ourselves, or the world and make changes for the better. But are you a peace warrior, an action hero warrior, a love warrior, an activist warrior, or a rebel warrior? Maybe you're a combination of them— like a love warrior latte with a shot of activist warrior. This quiz will help you find out, give you new ideas about how to be a warrior, and maybe inspire you to come up with other types of warriors that suit you.

All you have to do is pick which answer most resonates with you—and be sure to keep track of your answers on a piece of paper so you can tally them at the end (don't skip ahead and read the answer key or you

Quiz: What type of warrior are you?

will spoil the surprise)! And remember, there are no right or wrong answers here, only warriors!

1. If you see someone being bullied at school, work, or anywhere in your community, your first reaction is to:

   a. Confront the bully and try to defuse the situation nonviolently, or go get some help to stop the situation immediately.
   b. Wait until after the situation cools down, and then go comfort the person who was bullied.
   c. Become so upset at the sight of this bullying that you join a national anti-bullying campaign or start one in your community.
   d. Seek out the person who was doing the bullying and try to discover—in a compassionate way—what wound they have that makes them feel they need to hurt others.
   e. Assure the person who was bullied that they should not care what other people think of them. "Just ignore the bully and let the words roll off," is your advice. Life is too short to sit around worrying about other people's opinions of you.

2. You or a loved one is injured or diagnosed with an illness. Your initial impulse is:

   a. Start gathering all the information you can from experts about how to tackle this situation and begin a healing protocol ASAP.
   b. Take some time to be alone in nature and reflect on the bigger meaning of this illness or

continues

      injury—what it might teach you or how you should approach the situation philosophically.

c. Join a support group for other people who are affected or have family members affected by this condition to gain strength. Lobby the government or the medical community to do more for others in your situation.

d. Think about how this will affect you and your family emotionally. If this happens to a relative, you go into nurturing mode to take care of them. If this happens to you, you still go into nurturing mode, seeking out love from others and taking extra-good care of yourself.

e. Be smart about getting good traditional care, but also look for cutting-edge or alternative methods to help the healing process.

3. A romance or friendship ends, with the other person saying they no longer want to be a major part of your life. You:

a. Try to talk it out, find out how they are feeling, and see if there is a still a chance to save the relationship and change their mind. If the relationship really is over, you go to a party or concert or do some fun or meaningful activity with another friend to take your mind off things.

b. Listen to what the other person has to say with an open mind. You are curious to see yourself and this relationship from another person's perspective, or consider that maybe you have grown apart. You accept their decision as final and feel grateful for the time you had together.

   c. Realize that the loss of this relationship suddenly makes you feel compassion for people who are lonely. You befriend someone who seems like they do not have many friends or volunteer with people who are elderly and cannot get out of their homes to socialize.

   d. Have a good cry because this has broken a little piece of your heart (luckily your heart is so big). You immediately seek comfort from someone you love and trust, and after some time decide that you will always care for this person even if they no longer want to be in your life. You say good-bye but sincerely wish them well.

   e. Are hurt, but excited about the freedom this offers you, because you love not feeling tied down. You might stay single for a while, or find someone really unique and special to fill the role a friend is leaving.

4. You encounter a roadblock to something you want, like not getting into college, not being invited to join your friend's band, or being turned down for a part-time job you really thought would be fun. You:

   a. Immediately go into damage-control to find your next move. Tomorrow as soon as you get up, you'll make some calls and do some research so you can come up with a new plan to execute. After all, there's no time like the present!

   b. Are disappointed but not shocked. Sometimes we don't get what we want. But that only means there is something better on its way. You're sure if you wait and watch that something better will present itself.

continues

c. The injustice of it really gets to you. It's not fair that we can't all get what we want, because you deserved as much as anybody else to be at that college, in that band, or working that job. So, you take a few days to have a healthy sulk before picking yourself back up.

d. Mentally wish the other people well who got the opportunity. You're sure they worked hard and deserved it. Then you find someone to give you a big bear hug and maybe have a good, healing cry.

e. Realize that you did not want it as much as you originally thought. Instead of being part of the herd and going after what everyone else is going after, you'll look for an opportunity no one else is even interested in yet.

5. There's something you really want to try, but it's a bit of a stretch because you've never done it before—like getting a part in a play, finishing a marathon, or learning a new language—and you decide to go for it. Your first power move is to:

a. Practice, practice, practice. If you are trying out for a play, you get someone with theater experience to run lines with you. If you're signing up for a marathon, you hit the ground running—literally, and start training at once, running every day, researching training techniques, and even changing your diet. If you decide to learn a new language, you have some books and audio programs shipped to your house for overnight delivery.

Quiz: What type of warrior are you?

b. Get excited. What an adventure this will be! It doesn't matter whether you actually get the part, finish the marathon, or learn the language. You will definitely learn something and life will be way less boring. You start thinking of other new things you can try . . .

c. Find larger meaning in this journey. You choose a play about a cause close to your heart, find a marathon that allows you to raise money for medical research, or learn the language of a country in need where you can go and volunteer someday.

d. Tell yourself how proud you are that you are trying and stretching. To help calm your nerves, you remind yourself that you are beautiful, strong, talented, and lovable. You also reach out to friends to discuss how you are feeling and get a confidence boost.

e. Think of how you can accomplish this in a different way. You research experimental theater, try to find a skateboarding marathon, or dive into learning a language with a whole new alphabet.

Answer Key:

If you got mostly As . . . you are an action hero warrior! Roll up your sleeves, because if you're not doing something you are getting ready to do something. You like to meet life, goals, and challenges head on. You sometimes jump in feet first without looking, though, so try to do a little planning and impulse control. If something needs to be done, you are the person for the job, because you're great at making things happen. Remind yourself to slow down,

continues

though, so you can sit back and savor your accomplish-
ments. You see the cup as half full and always feel there is
a chance at victory, which is why you try so hard and put
your whole self into your efforts.

Your warrior superpower: Bringing hope and optimism to
the world and inspiring others with your achievements.

Action hero warriors in pop culture: LeBron James, Rich-
ard Branson, Oprah

*If you got mostly Bs . . . you are a **peace warrior!*** Picture
someone chilling out in the lotus pose . . . that's your favorite attitude. You're great at surrendering and looking at life
as a fascinating adventure, and not being reactive or taking
other people's bait. You're also aces at avoiding unnecessary drama and taking a philosophical attitude to setbacks.
However, peaceful does not always mean passive. Don't
let anyone take advantage of your easygoing attitude, and
if you really want something, fight for it.

Your warrior superpower: Showing the world that strength
can be steady and calm and teaching others nonattachment through your example.

Peace warriors in pop culture: Deepak Chopra, Tina
Turner, the Dalai Lama

*If you got mostly Cs . . . you are an **activist warrior!*** Injustice, watch out, there's a new sheriff in town. You don't
wait for someone else to tell you what is right and wrong—
you feel it in your gut. Especially when someone is being

Quiz: What type of warrior are you?

treated unfairly. Do your part to change the world, but realize you will never change everything and everyone you disagree with. Focus on the good you can do and know that every small step toward more equality and compassion counts, big time.

Your warrior superpower: Acting as the conscience of the world and encouraging others to take care of each other and the planet.

Activist warriors in pop culture: Malala Yousafzai, Bill and Melinda Gates, Leonardo DiCaprio, Amal Clooney

*If you got mostly Ds . . . you are a **love warrior!*** It hurts you to see other people or animals hurting, because you can actually feel their emotions. You are sensitive and possess a big heart and can look at a situation from many perspectives. This makes you a natural diplomat. Just don't become a natural doormat. Have strong emotional boundaries so you can live grounded and in your own skin.

Your warrior superpower: Bringing more unconditional love and acceptance into the world, especially to those people who are wounded, in conflict, or need it most.

Love warriors in pop culture: Ellen DeGeneres, Van Jones, Dolly Parton

*If you answered mostly Es . . . you are a **rebel warrior!*** But you probably already knew that! Rebels are hard to miss . . . they are always doing the unexpected, cutting-edge stuff. Walking on the wild side is something you like

continues

Quiz: What type of warrior are you?   *continued*

to do every single day. Only make sure that your need to be nonconformist does not cause you to miss out on things you really want to do just because they fall into the "normal" category. Never judge a book by its cover, and you are often a walking contradiction—which means you are always interesting. You are good at seeing people for who they are and like to have friends of all different personality types and backgrounds.

Your warrior superpower: Blazing your own trail, being a visionary, and showing others that they should be true to their individuality.

Rebel warriors in pop culture: Peter Dinklage, JAY-Z, Lady Gaga, Laverne Cox

Warrior wrap-up: Sometimes friends and family know us better than we know ourselves, so if you're unsure what type of warrior you are after taking this quiz, ask the people closest to you what they think. You can play a fun game with your intuition to receive answers, too: ask your higher self which type of warrior best describes you, and wait for an answer. You might hear "peace warrior" in your mind or get an image of an iconic rebel you've always admired. And don't forget that you might have a little of all of these warrior types inside you!

22

Open Your Heart

Why it works: Your heart is gentle, nurturing, and forgiving. When you are stressed, it can be helpful to be gentle with yourself, nurture yourself, and forgive yourself.

The heart has its own wisdom and answers the head could never guess. Your heart actually speaks to you through your emotions, gut instincts, and the feelings you get about situations, places, and people. Your heart is probably telling you something right now. Heart messages include: slow down and take better care of yourself; forgive or accept someone else or yourself; speak up for what you believe in; spend more time with the people you love; dream big; make a difference; notice the magic in nature; be of service to others; feel all your feelings—even the challenging ones; love yourself unconditionally.

There are times when it can be useful to purposefully connect with your heart and its wisdom, like when you are disappointed, when you are confused, when you are heartbroken, when you have a tough decision to make, when you want to navigate a sticky situation, when you are so angry at someone you can't see straight, when you feel betrayed, before you ask someone an important question, or when you are feeling scared or vulnerable. Messages from the heart are always healing and will help you discern the truth from your conflicting emotions (sometimes all that anger is masking a lot of hurt, and sometimes part of your anxiety is really excitement).

A philosophical perspective: Life works best when there is co-operation, or synergy, between the heart and the head. The intellectual side of you, which is practical, logical, loves to strategize, and makes sure your material needs are met, is just as important as your heart, which is more concerned with emotions, giving to others, your spirituality, and your sixth sense, or intuition.

Make it work for you: There are many ways to open your heart:

1. Get quiet, put your hand over your heart, and ask silently, "What would my heart say right now?"
2. Watch your favorite sappy movie.
3. Listen to a song that always touches your heart and makes you feel very emotional.
4. Look through old photos.
5. Call up a friend who lives far away for a heart-to-heart chat.
6. Watch a viral video of puppies or babies, or better yet puppies playing with babies.
7. Take a walk in nature to make contact with something larger than yourself that you are still a part of.
8. Write a list of five things/people you are really grateful for and then stick it to your bathroom mirror.
9. Have a good cry about something in your own life, or something happening in the world, that is upsetting you.
10. Ask a friend or family member for a hug.
11. Donate time or money to a cause you believe in.
12. Buy yourself or someone else flowers.
13. Write a note to your future self (five years from now) telling yourself that no matter what, you are so proud of *you* (then

put the note somewhere safe where you will find it by surprise much later).

14. Give someone a random compliment.

15. Look yourself in the mirror and sincerely tell yourself, "I
love you."

16. Write a close friend, favorite teacher, or family member
(sibling, cousin, foster parent, etc.) a note telling them what
you most enjoy and admire about them.

17. Spend time with a pet or small child.

18. Tell someone "thank you" from the bottom of your heart.

19. Go out of your way to do something nice for someone else.

Tips on how opening your heart feels:

An open heart is **expansive.**

An open heart is **compassionate.**

An open heart is **curious.**

An open heart is **in touch with *all* its emotions.**

An open heart is **honest,** even when it hurts.

An open heart is **merciful.**

An open heart is **hopeful.**

An open heart is **protective.**

An open heart is **vulnerable.**

An open heart is **accepting.**

An open heart is **wise.**

An open heart is **treating others the way you would want to
be treated.**

The magical side of an open heart: Touching base with your
heart is its own wonderful kind of magic, since the heart is both a
living organ that pumps blood through our bodies and a symbol

of our connection to the more noble, forgiving, and caring side of ourselves.

The shadow side of an open heart: Opening your heart can make you feel vulnerable. If you are afraid of opening yourself to others, remember that having an open heart does not mean you must let someone hurt you or someone you love. Having an open heart means staying open to what is good in others while maintaining healthy boundaries and expecting that others treat you with respect and kindness, just as you try to treat them. Check in with your heart if you are confused, hurt, or stuck—but also consult your head for some grounded, logical advice. The best decisions are made with the head *and* the heart.

Give it a try: A great way to open your heart is by being kinder to yourself and others. One way to be kinder is to be more patient. Remember that becoming more patient takes practice, so try not to get impatient with your own attempts to become more patient!

Exercise:

Step 1. Get out your journal so you can tap into the wisdom of an open heart by asking your heart some basic questions about a challenge you are currently facing. Pick a situation in your life to focus on.

Step 2. Place your hand over your heart and sit quietly for a minute or two to help you connect with your heart. Imagine a bubble of warm, soft, gentle energy forming around you where you sit. Picture this bubble of unconditional love and acceptance coming from your own heart.

Step 3. Have a heart-to-heart chat with your own heart. Here are a few journal prompts to get you started: What is the deeper purpose or lesson this situation holds for me? How am I making this experience harder on myself than it needs to be? Who have I misjudged? Who could be most helpful to me right now? Who or what is adding to the drama and should be avoided? How can I comfort or be gentle with myself right now? Who can I turn to for solid advice? How can I be kinder to myself during this experience?

Step 4. Write down your heart's advice in your journal.

23

Experience Heart Healing

W hy it works: Heart healing is a simple prescription—it's just about doing healthy things that make you feel good.

There are times when we all need a little heart healing. Maybe you are scared about a natural disaster or a family member who is away in the military. End-of-semester tests and deadlines might have left your body run-down and your nervous system as frazzled as curly hair on a hot, humid day. Perhaps you had a big blowup with a good friend and you're feeling confused and vulnerable. You might be going through big changes, like your parents announcing that the whole family is moving to another state, or maybe you are moving out on your own after high school. Heart healing is what we call those healthy things we turn to again and again for comfort and nourishment.

Do you have a favorite television show or movie where the characters are kind, and even though they have problems everything works out in the end? Maybe you've seen this show or movie several times before and it always makes you feel peaceful and reassured. That's one for your chest of heart healing treasures! Is there a place you like to go that always cheers you up? Maybe it's the same walk in nature or one of your favorite coffee shops or museums. You might have been on this path or to this coffee shop a hundred times. And it's exactly because this place is familiar that it's such good heart healing. Doing your favorite activities, like spending a whole afternoon practicing your bass or shooting hoops with a friend, can be excellent heart healing. Wearing your favorite clothes or eating your favorite snack can also be heart healing. Calling up an old friend, or making a date to hang out in person, can be some of the best heart healing of all. Heart healing is about spending time with those things, places, people, and activities we always enjoy—it's like reminding ourselves what is always true about us.

A philosophical perspective:

Heart healing is about nurturing and being gentle with yourself. The heart can take a lot, but it's also sensitive. If you've been going through a bunch of drama or intense or harsh life experiences lately, the heart might need some extra healing (not your physical heart, but the energetic heart we discussed in the last section). You'll know that something is good heart healing because you will feel calmer, safer, and more reflective after a dose of it. Heart healing makes you feel closer to yourself and others. Heart healing should also make you feel like being kinder and less judgmental toward yourself and others. That's because when we feed the energetic heart with healing, that part of ourselves expands—just as anything we feed expands.

Make it work for you:

You don't always have to wait until your heart is hurting or tired to administer heart healing! Once you get used to the idea, you might find yourself seeking out heart healing on a regular basis, just like you might take supplements or medicine on a regular basis. In time, you will also start to get better at recognizing heart healing. Maybe you spend the summer on an art project, and afterward tell a friend, "This was such good heart healing!" Or you might put together a big puzzle over the holiday break with your little brother, and as you high five each other after placing the last piece, you realize that the experience was great heart healing for you both.

Tips for getting a dose of heart healing:

Watch a video or read a news article about people doing something kind for those in need, animals, or the environment.

Treat yourself to something (it does not have to cost a lot, or any, money).

Make a list of five ways you could be kinder to yourself.

Ask someone for advice.

Whenever you hear a mean or judgmental thought about yourself in your mind, tell yourself silently: "I love you, and I know you're doing the best you can."

Give someone the benefit of the doubt.

Tell someone who you know looks up to you something you admire about *them*.

Listen to your favorite gentle music with heartfelt lyrics.

Take a break from shows, video games, and books that contain violence.

Spend more time outdoors and less time in front of a screen.

Ask someone you care about if there's something on their mind, and be fully present and paying close attention when they answer.

Get lost in a creative project.

Slow down and take the long way home.

Forgive yourself for something that has been bugging you.

Set aside an afternoon to hang with one of your favorite people, face-to-face.

Set aside an afternoon to work on your favorite hobby.

Go to a place—like a record store or coffee shop or community center or church or skate park—where everyone knows you.

Spend time with an animal.

Spend time with a small child.

Reread one of your favorite books.

Cook one of your favorite meals.

Start a project with a friend or sibling that you work on together regularly.

Tend a garden.

Snuggle up with a blanket or pet.

Join a volunteer group with people who share your values.

Ask a close friend what they most admire and love about you.

Write a list in your journal of things you most love and admire about yourself.

The magical side of heart healing: You are unique, so what feels like heart healing to you will also be unique. In time, you'll develop a whole list of things that are guaranteed heart healing for you!

The shadow side of heart healing: Too much of a good thing can be not so good anymore. Avoid the temptation to get lost in a person or activity that feels like heart healing yet causes you to neglect your responsibilities. Heart healing should help you balance life. Heart healing is not an excuse to hide away from our problems or our pain. Rather it is a way to soothe us no matter what is happening in our lives and a way to provide healthy breaks and escape.

Give it a try: Get out your journal and write down some familiar activities that always make you feel kinder, softer, happier, and more nurtured. Then see how many of these you can incorporate into your life this week! How does experiencing more heart healing change the way you view your life and the world?

24

Harness the Tao of Cool

Why it works: Things that initially appear to be complex can actually be quite simple, and the secret to being cool can be boiled down to this: *Being cool means not caring what other people think of you.* It's simple, straightforward, and true. There's just one catch: You have to *honestly* not care what others think. So, the most important person you need to convince of your coolness is you.

If you're worrying about how other people see you or feeling anxious about the opinions of others, work on your own sense of cool. Start with self-love, and think about all the things you like about yourself: your compassionate heart; your sense of humor; your style; your taste in books, movies, and music; any talents you have in math, science, theater, sports, music, writing, public speaking, computers and tech stuff, painting, dance, pottery, working with animals, or working with children.

If you are feeling self-conscious about your physical appearance, concentrate on just one thing that you love about your body—just one is all you need to jump-start more self-acceptance. Then thank your body for being an amazing vehicle for your soul. Your body isn't perfect. Maybe there is something you wish you could change about your physical appearance, or maybe your body has some real limitations. Try to have gratitude for this body, which helps your soul experience life, and you'll begin to accept and respect even the parts of your body that you don't always like. (Maybe something you had trouble accepting about your physical appearance will end up making you famous, like Canadian model Winnie Harlow's skin condition, vitiligo.) Also, make a list of what is most unique about you—those particular character traits will always be your keys to what is coolest about you. Being cool is ultimately about owning yourself—all of yourself.

A philosophical perspective:
How you treat yourself can influence how others treat you. Make it a game by developing a healthy self-image and tuning the haters out. The person's opinion that should mean the most to you is always your own, but negative opinions of others can challenge our self-worth if we let them. Keep telling yourself that those opinions do not define your coolness, your identity, your potential, or your self-worth. If someone doesn't approve of you, then rebel against their opinion. Being a rebel is always cool!

Make it work for you:
The best chance you have at being cool is always being your authentic self. If you genuinely like what someone else is doing or wearing, find a way to make these things your own. But trying to copy someone else just to be cool never really works. Every human is one unique piece of a giant jigsaw puzzle, so no two pieces are alike. The best chance you have of fitting in is by owning and honoring your own special shape.

The magical side of cool:
Cultivating cool can get you more in touch with your true self and help you develop more self-love.

The shadow side of cool:
Cultivate cool, don't chase it. If you chase after cool by trying too hard to become something you aren't, cool will elude you or run away.

Your Zen master's legit list tips, or how to attain coolness:

1. If you believe you are cool, the rest will follow.

2. Remember that cool is subjective. Not everyone will think you're cool, just like you won't always think others are cool.

3. Trends come and go, but people truly cool are timeless.

Aretha Franklin	Jack Kerouac
Art Spiegelman	Jackie Robinson
Audrey Hepburn	Jim Henson
Bob Marley	Joan of Arc
Bruce Lee	Johnny Cash
Coco Chanel	Lily Tomlin
David Bowie	Maya Angelou
Deborah Harry	Michael Jordan
Frida Kahlo	Mozart
George Lucas	Nelson Mandela
Ghandi	Rimbaud
Harvey Milk	Rosa Parks
Ian MacKaye	Rumi
Iggy Pop	Salvador Dali
J. K. Rowling	Spike Lee
J. R. R. Tolkien	

Remember, just recognizing that one of these people is cool makes you cool, too.

Your Zen master's legit list tips

4. You don't have to be perfect to be cool. Take a look at that list of timelessly cool people again. They all made mistakes and had regrets. They are all flawed, imperfectly cool people.

5. Nonattachment (or not caring so much about outcomes and going with the flow) is the height of cool.

6. Reflect on what is most unique about you—those are also the things that are coolest about you!

Give it a try: When you stop caring about what others think so much, your cool factor increases and your stress factor decreases. Practice being incredibly chill and relaxed in social situations for one week . . . watch how your cool ranking rises with yourself and others, and notice how much calmer you feel.

Then write in your journal a list of what is most unique about you, and also what you most admire about yourself (it might help to think about what you get complimented on the most by people you respect). This will increase self-love and magically make you more magnetic to others!

25

Work with Vision Boards

Why it works: Wouldn't it be great to have a visual reminder of your dreams, goals, and everything you love about life? That's exactly what a vision board is, and the images and words on them provide clarity, focus, and inspiration. You can find items for your board online and in magazines and newspapers—anything that's visual and inspires you will work. Here are a few items you can include on your board:

Inspiring quotes and words
Images of dream destinations
Photos of friends and family
Reminders of fun activities
Images of characters you admire from books or television
Drawings that make you smile
Lists of intentions and goals
Colors that invigorate you (see pages 31–34 for more about the
    power of colors)
Gurus who inspire you (see pages 6–9 for more about gurus)
Interesting or beautiful objects like feathers or ribbons

When you assemble these positive cues in one place, they create a visual reminder of all the things that make you happy, fulfilled, and hopeful about your present and future.

A philosophical perspective: Vision boards are a great way to connect with yourself. When you look at your board, it should be, in a way, like looking in the mirror. Vision boards also act as a tool to help you prioritize. Sometimes we don't meet our goals because we aren't clear on what we really want or what is truly important to us. Vision boards are daily reminders of what you want *more* of in your life. Think of it as a visual diary.

Make it work for you: Your vision board represents your personal vision for your life. You can change it anytime, just like you can decide to change or begin shifting aspects of your life. If you've outgrown something on your vision board, or if something on your vision board no longer seems inspiring, don't be afraid to switch it up. When you walk by or glance at your board, it should make you feel happy and motivated.

The magical side of vision boards: Vision boards can be a symbolic way to let go of things you have outgrown or revise your dreams as time goes on. Dreams and goals are living things that evolve all the time, just like humans. As you evolve, so will your vision board.

The shadow side of vision boards: Putting something on a vision board won't make it come true; it's only a first step to manifesting what you want. Most of the time you will have to take action to enjoy the things you love, bring your dreams into reality, and achieve your goals. And many times your dreams and goals will show up in unexpected ways and forms in your life. So your vision board is just a starting point.

Give it a try: Create a themed vision board. You can do this on a piece of corkboard, with Pinterest, or through an app you get for your phone. Focus on one topic, and fill your board with images and words that are meaningful to you. Try a topic of your own, or one of these:

1. "Stuff That Keeps Me Chill"
2. "Stuff That Makes Me Glad to Be Alive"
3. "The Way I Want to Feel Is . . ."
4. "Things I Want to Do When I Get out of High School"
5. "Dream Careers"
6. "People I Admire"
7. "Stuff I Want to Try"
8. "Things I Want to Learn More About"
9. "Places I Want to Go"
10. "Stuff I Want to Get Better At"
11. "I'm Proud of Myself Because . . ."
12. "My Favorite Places in Nature"
13. "Where I'm Headed in Life"
14. "What Makes Me . . . Me!"

26

Take Satisfying Shavasana Breaks

Why it works: Shavasana breaks are like taking a relaxing nap without going to sleep.

Shavasana—a yoga pose lying still, flat on your back—is also known as "corpse pose," but don't let that scare you! The name simply describes how peaceful this pose is. The goal of the shavasana break is to enter a state of deep relaxation. Not only is this calming for the body, it calms the mind and the nervous system. It's typically included at the end of yoga classes, but you don't have to take a yoga class to enjoy the benefits of shavasana.

Some people like to listen to nature sounds or chants during shavasana pose, others will place a lavender eye pillow over their faces to help them relax, and others will try to make their minds blank or go into a guided meditation.

A philosophical perspective: Practicing shavasana breaks not only calms your body in the moment, it trains both the body and mind to remain still throughout the day. After several weeks of taking daily shavasana breaks, you might find yourself watching television or reading a book for a whole hour straight and barely moving, instead of your normal routine: getting up to check your phone, going to the bathroom, grabbing a snack, or just shifting position every few minutes. You might also notice that your mental focus and concentration increase as well, so that you get more out of the book or movie you are enjoying.

Make it work for you: To enter shavasana pose, stretch out on a carpeted floor or on top of a thick rug or lay down on a few fluffy beach towels or a yoga mat. The traditional way to do corpse pose is by lying flat on your back with arms and legs also lying flat against the floor about a foot away from your torso. But the golden rule in yoga is to do what feels comfortable. So, if you find it more relaxing to lay your hands on your stomach, turn your head to the side, or any other variation on traditional corpse pose, go for it! If your body doesn't easily lie flat on the floor, no problem! Just get into the most comfortable position for *you*. If you are already a yoga rock star, you know that one of the most challenging aspects of corpse pose is to remain still. Not only trying to still the mind as we do in meditation, but trying to keep the body from fidgeting or changing position. This takes practice, and again, if you have a condition that makes it hard for you to remain totally still physically, concentrate on trying to still your mind or slow and deepen your breath. Once you can train your body to lie still or take a break for ten or fifteen minutes, you'll notice the benefits even after you get up off the floor.

You can take a shavasana break anytime you can find a quiet moment alone to spend ten or fifteen minutes powering down. Just like computers sometimes need to reboot or restart, shavasana breaks are a way you can reset your psychical and mental systems at the beginning, end, or middle of the day.

Tips on perfect times to slip into shavasana pose:

When: Right before you leave the house for work or school in the morning.

Why? So you start the day calm and centered.

When: After you first walk in the door at home in the evening/afternoon from work or school.

Why? To reinforce that work and school are over and now you will be fully present at home to your personal life.

When: Midday.

Why? To break up the day and recharge for the afternoon.

When: In the middle of studying for a big exam.

Why? To reset your brain (like rebooting a computer).

When: If you are feeling especially emotional—worried, angry, anxious, or sad.

Why? To calm your nervous system, gain perspective, and allow for a break from the intensity of your feelings.

The magical side of shavasana pose: It's totally free! You don't need anything but you—and a quiet, private place—to take advantage of shavasana pose. If you love attending yoga class or doing yoga at home, remember that you can enter shavasana pose at any time without doing other poses first.

The shadow side of shavasana pose: If you are super tired, it will be tough to take advantage of shavasana pose—you might end up falling asleep!

Give it a try: Spend fifteen minutes in shavasana pose. Notice the effects on your mind and body, both during the pose and afterward.

27

Embrace Loving-Kindness

Why it works: The idea of expressing love through acts of kindness is popular in many spiritual traditions and cultures. When you think of being kind or expressing affection, who do you imagine as the recipient of this blessing? Maybe someone in need or suffering, a pet, a good friend, or an elderly relative or neighbor. For a moment, let's focus on extending loving-kindness to someone who can always use and appreciate it—ourselves.

The way we treat others is often a mirror for how we treat ourselves. If you know someone who can be harsh, critical, and unforgiving with others, they are probably very judgmental and unforgiving with themselves in their own mind and heart. So the best place to begin changing the world for the better is from the inside out. Practicing loving-kindness on ourselves strengthens our roots so that we can grow tall and strong like a giant tree, providing shade and shelter to others.

A philosophical perspective: Imagine that you have a fuel or battery gauge, like the ones in cars. But instead of displaying how much gasoline or battery power you have, this fuel gauge shows how much you have in reserve to give to others physically and emotionally. There may be times when you are feeling great, getting lots of rest, and things in your life are flowing along smoothly. During these periods you might be inspired to give more to others:

more advice, more help, more love, more time, more compassion. Your fuel gauge is reading full. But when you are drained and tired; you're facing major challenges; you have a lot of commitments; or you are feeling vulnerable, scared, or stressed, you won't have as much loving-kindness to give away to others. Your fuel gauge is showing you are closer to empty, and you need to concentrate on extending loving-kindness to yourself.

Make it work for you: Part of extending loving-kindness to yourself means putting yourself first. This is not an excuse to be selfish or act cruelly to others, but a reminder that the best person to look out for your interests or nurture and protect you is always . . . you. Waiting around for someone else to anticipate your needs or desires or take care of you can be a big waste of time. Speak up and ask for help, but also take responsibility for your own health and happiness.

The magical side of loving-kindness: When we practice loving-kindness with ourselves or anyone else, it expands our hearts and deepens our ability to feel compassion for others, whether it's someone down the street from us or on the other side of the world. And this planet needs more compassion.

The shadow side of loving-kindness: Not everyone may naturally inspire loving-kindness in you. Pick someone at school, at work, or in your community who seems mean or cold. You don't have to approach or interact with them to extend them loving-kindness. Simply close your eyes and spend a few minutes wishing them well, sending them good vibes, or imagining wrapping them in a warm, golden blanket of love. See if this changes or softens the way you feel about them—or even yourself!

Give it a try:

Step 1. Get quiet and tune into your body and emotions to see where your own fuel gauge is right now. This might take a minute.

Step 2. Is your tank only half full or are you running on empty? If so, concentrate on loving-kindness toward yourself. If your tank is full or almost full, go out and practice some random acts of loving-kindness on others.

Step 3. Repeat this exercise once a week or once a month. It helps to not only encourage loving-kindness, but checking in with your own fuel gauge can let you know if you are feeling stressed, overwhelmed, or run-down.

If each of us gave ourselves loving-kindness when our tanks were empty and showed loving-kindness to others when our tanks were full, there would always be enough loving-kindness to go around!

Tips and tricks for showing yourself loving-kindness:

Get in the habit of quietly asking yourself, "What do I need most right now?" After stopping to ponder this question with an open mind, you might realize you most need to get to bed an hour earlier each night, or limit your time with a certain friend who doesn't have the same goals or concerns as you or isn't very accepting and supportive. Maybe you just need to grab a bottle of your favorite kombucha or sing along to your favorite song in the shower.

Allow yourself to say "no" to things, like one more extra-curricular activity when your schedule is already packed, or one more shift at your job when you need more spare time to follow a dream or just relax with friends.

Make sure you have lunches that are healthy AND tasty. This might involve a little planning ahead at home and the grocery store, but it's an excellent and yummy way to nurture yourself.

Make space to cry, journal, have a heart-to-heart chat with a friend, or express yourself in some way when you are feeling sad. Taking care of yourself when you are hurt will make you feel safe and protected.

Admit when someone has crossed your boundaries. Whether a friend said something unkind about you or someone you care about, or you feel you are being treated unfairly at home, school, or work, it's important to stop and acknowledge, at least to yourself, that someone crossed your healthy boundaries. Take some time to think the experience over, and talk to someone you trust, to help you decide how to best deal with the situation.

Schedule an afternoon of "me time" in a no-stress zone. Sometimes there just isn't enough of "you" to go around, and you have to hoard it all for yourself! Spend an afternoon snuggling up with a good book, rewatching a favorite movie, working on a creative project, taking a walk in nature, going for a run, starting a sewing project, baking a cake, jamming on an instrument, riding your skateboard, soaking in the tub as you listen to an insightful podcast, or putting together a photo album. You'll feel renewed and refreshed afterward! The only rules are: No stress!

Tips and tricks for showing others loving-kindness:

Smile and say thank you to cashiers.

Offer to do a chore for someone who is elderly.

Text a funny GIF to a friend who has been feeling down.

Send an email telling a friend that no matter what happens, you will always love them.

Surprise your parents or roommate by making dinner.

Go out of your way to hold the door or elevator open for someone.

Be kind to someone who seems like they don't have many friends.

Invite someone who has been having a rough time at home to your house for dinner and make it a fun, special night.

Give a friend or sibling a hug if they have been stressed or anxious about something, and hold on to them for a few seconds longer than you normally would.

Volunteer your time to a needy cause.

Donate clothes you have outgrown or things you no longer use.

Make a positive impact on the planet by looking for ways you can reduce the waste you and your family produce.

Find a child in your life who could use some extra attention and become a mentor, friend, or advocate for them.

Refrain from gossip, especially if what you are telling others is a secret or might hurt someone's feelings.

Wish someone well who appears really mean or cold (you can do this silently by sending loving vibes their way).

Look for ways to be a force of love and compassion in the world.

Be patient with someone who is trying their best but normally frustrates you.

Inspire people with your life, by simply being more loving and kind to yourself and others.

Encourage others to be kind to themselves.

Show mercy to others when you can to be a force of grace in the world.

28

Go on a Digital Detox

Why it works: Sometimes a part of our lives that was productive or positive becomes addictive or self-sabotaging, and we need to step away temporarily to regain balance. You might have experienced this if an exercise regime or diet that was once healthy and stress-relieving became, over time, obsessive or punishing.

> Have you ever heard the word "sabbatical"? It comes from the term "Sabbath," or the Judeo-Christian day of rest (typically observed on a Saturday or Sunday). According to the dictionary, a sabbatical is "a break or change from a normal routine." And taking a sabbatical from something—even things you love—can rejuvenate your energy, calm your nervous system, and give you a fresh perspective.

Temporary sabbaticals help curb extreme behaviors, and our daily connections to digital devices are almost always extreme. From the moment we wake up to the time we go to sleep, our phones, computers, tablets, and other devices inform us, guide us, and entertain us. That's just a little too much togetherness for any healthy relationship.

A philosophical perspective: It can be wise to unplug and take intentional breaks from the modern world of television, video games, and social media—or all things digital. Everyone will have a different threshold or tolerance for digital consumption. If you want to design video games someday, you'll naturally watch more of them than some of your friends. If you want to be a storyteller, you will probably have seen many movies your friends haven't found time for. But in a world where everyone is trying to get your attention with a digital offering, taking a daylong or even weeklong sabbatical can help you decide what's really worth your attention.

Make it work for you: After you come back from your digital break (don't worry, you are supposed to come back!) you'll realize that some of the videos or posts you were spending time on were actually a waste of your time. Instead of saving you from feeling bored, this digital "content" was probably making your boredom worse. During your unplugging sabbatical, you will likely get back in touch with things you enjoy that have nothing to do with digital content, like interacting with people and animals, playing sports, spending time in nature, reading a book, cooking, or starting a creative project. The next time you are bored you'll remember that you don't have to plug in to be entertained. Simply engaging face-to-face with life, as opposed to escaping into digital content, is very entertaining.

The magical side of unplugging: Your day will seem a lot longer and you'll have more free time when you aren't constantly checking social media or glued to some kind of screen. This sense of more time will make you feel relaxed, as well as help you be more productive and reflective about your own life, needs, patterns, and goals.

Benefits of unplugging include:

Resets the body's **circadian cycle** or **natural rhythm**.
Increases **concentration and focus**.
Encourages **face-to-face communication**.
Emphasizes **balance**.
Helps prioritize **time and resources**.
Helps distinguish which digital content is **nourishing**.
Encourages being **present** to yourself and your **feelings**.
Encourages being **present** with **other people**.
Gives the nervous system and eyes a **rest**.

The shadow side of unplugging: Don't be tempted to think that enjoying social media or binge-watching your favorite show is bad. Modern technology is a blessing that can make the world a better, more informed, and compassionate place (think of all the social activism and awareness that can be accomplished via digital tools). Because of the digital revolution, we live in a very exciting time.

Give it a try:

Step 1. One Saturday or Sunday, set aside a whole afternoon for a digital sabbatical and go offline.

Step 2. If you start to feel bored (which is normal), see where that boredom takes you. Sit through the initial frustration and you'll probably think of something interesting to do that does not involve a computer, like organizing your desk, creating a vision board, taking a walk in nature, meditating, spending time with a sibling, meeting up with a friend, reading a book, baking a cake, writing in your journal, or starting a creative project.

Step 3. Look back over the day and see if you can work more of the activities you did offline into your daily life. Was there something you did you had forgotten you like—such as spending the afternoon riding your bike or taking your dog on a long walk?

Step 4. For the week ahead, keep a digital logbook in your journal. Just record how many hours each day you spent watching television, playing video games, texting on your phone, posting or sharing on social media, or surfing online. With so much digital content and devices available, sometimes people are not aware of their digital consumption until they see it written down in black and white.

29

Cultivate Gratitude

W**hy it works:** Gratitude reminds you what you love about life and why even the hard times are worth it.

Probably the best time to work on gratitude is when you feel *least* grateful, because that's when you need it most. An attitude of gratitude is a great way to turn around a sour or funky mood (some funks are groovy, like in music, but with moods and leftovers, funk ain't good). Start small with gratitude, because everything is easier and more manageable when you start small. You could just be thankful for the sky above your head or the ground beneath your feet. Then expand that out to feeling grateful for whatever cool natural wonders are near your home. Maybe you live by majestic mountains that inspire you with their views, a killer beach that calms you with its rhythmic waves, thick woods that make you feel like fairies are around every corner, or just a great park or community garden. Being grateful for the earth helps us to live green and take better care of our planet's resources.

Next, think about something unique to you or your life that you are grateful for. Maybe you and a sibling have been getting closer lately (though fighting over chores is still allowed); you might have discovered you have a rare talent for singing or playing guitar; you could have earned a scholarship that will pay for some of your expenses at the private school of your dreams; maybe you were hanging with a group that was negative or even violent and you recently broke free; you might have learned some new, safe tricks on your skateboard and in the process realized that skating helps keep you chill; possibly your parents have been fighting a lot and you found a safe place to escape the drama like a friend's house or a community center or even getting lost in a great creative project; or perhaps you have struggled with an eating disorder and are finally starting to make progress, feel healthier, and love your body unconditionally. *No matter what is going on in your life, you have things to be grateful for.*

A philosophical perspective: Gratitude can make you appreciate life more and help you be more present to all the good stuff when it's actually happening, instead of ignoring it, taking it for granted, or spending all your time focusing on what you don't have or what you want to change about your life. It's awesome to go after new goals and dreams and change things that aren't working in your life, but balance that with being grateful for what *is* working in your life.

Make it work for you: An attitude of gratitude increases feelings of peace and joy and is a first-rate way of putting life in perspective if you feel like everything is going wrong or life is against you. Thinking about what you want but don't have can be motivating, but if you focus on what is lacking in your life all the time it quickly becomes depressing. When people are depressed, their energy levels and motivation typically go way down, which makes it harder to go after their dreams or change their lives for the better. So always focusing on what you want but do not have is kind of a vicious circle, like a dog chasing its tail—very unproductive.

The magical side of cultivating gratitude: Being grateful helps you see your life from a more objective perspective. When you look at things from an objective perspective it helps you see situations for what they really are, as your emotions are not getting in the way.

The shadow side of cultivating gratitude: Don't force yourself to feel grateful for things that are hurtful or broken in your life. If something in your life is not functioning well, pay attention to your feelings and don't pretend "it's all good" when it isn't. Acknowledging what isn't working in your life helps you process your emotions and inspires you to make changes for the better.

Grow your gratitude:

Be grateful you are alive: Some people, maybe even someone you know and love, did not get to make it to the age you're at right now. Be grateful you are still in the game of life. (If your life circumstances are making it difficult for you to feel grateful for simply being alive, don't worry—your circumstances will change for the better. And don't be afraid to ask for help and support along the way!)

Be grateful you can read: If you are reading this book, count your blessings. Many people never got the chance to learn how to read.

Be grateful that you are loved: Someone in your life loves you very much—you! Other people also care. Close your eyes and picture the face of someone who loves you.

Be grateful for the good times: We've all experienced the bad times, so make the good times count. Celebrate the easy, fun, heartwarming moments. They will last longer that way!

> Grow your gratitude
>
> **Be grateful that you can change:** The only person you have any real power over is yourself, but you can change several aspects of your life—not everything, but plenty of stuff. Pretty exciting, right?
>
> **Be grateful for the lessons:** Even hard times have their silver linings—lessons we take with us to improve our lives and share with others. What hard-won wisdom have you picked up from getting through a difficult situation?
>
> **Be grateful for what gets you through challenges:** If you were diagnosed with cancer, you might work on feeling grateful for your medicine and your doctors.
>
> **Be grateful for grace and mercy:** On your travels through existence, you will find that some things just come to you, like little gifts from life. Grace and mercy do not have to be earned, just received or accepted, like signing for a present that comes in the mail.

Give it a try: Create a gratitude jar:

Step 1. Find an attractive receptacle for all your gratitude. It could be a plain blue mason jar, a piece of pottery that a relative made, or a bowl from your kitchen. Keep your gratitude jar displayed somewhere obvious, like on your desk or bedside table, so you notice it.

Step 2. Place a small pad of paper and a pen or pencil by the jar. Every time you think of something you are grateful for, you can write it down on a slip of paper. Then tear that paper off, fold it over, and place it inside your gratitude jar.

Step 3. When you're feeling down, you can read these slips of gratitude to remind yourself of all the blessings in your life and savor some good memories. That will cheer you up—promise!

Step 4. See if anyone else in your house wants to contribute to the gratitude jar!

PART 5

Habits to Keep You Happy & Healthy

30

Be Present

Why it works: People often accuse those who grew up in the digital age of being less present. "They're always on their phones!" someone might claim. It's true there are more ways to be distracted now than ever—you can binge-watch Netflix or YouTube, scroll through social media, or play your favorite video game (some of those distractions actually sound good right about now). Yet not being present doesn't really have anything *specifically* to do with computers or technology.

Not being present is about taking yourself out of the moment. If you are posting an Instagram picture of your family on vacation and enjoying seeing all the responses flood in, sounds like you are very present in the moment. But have you ever found yourself surfing the web for an hour—visiting shopping sites, reading celebrity gossip, and scanning social media feeds—without taking away anything interesting or of substance? In these cases, it's almost like you were a zombie sleepwalking through that hour (although without the cool ability to slowly move toward friends and family in a creepy and terrifying fashion). This is what it means to not be present—to zone out, space out, or tune out.

We all need downtime and healthy ways to escape. The trick is finding healthy ways to escape where you actually stay *more* present—like watching a great documentary on a cause you care about or checking out the film version of one of your favorite books. Being present means being engaged, and when people are engaged—interested, entertained, excited, concerned, and everything else that is the opposite of bored—they are aware of what is going on and what they are taking in.

A philosophical perspective: Life is short. None of us really knows how long we will be here. Being present is about recognizing that you have limited time on this planet and appreciating the individual moments within the experiences life has given you. When we don't, we miss out on people, opportunities, conversations, memories, and feelings that we'll never be able to get back. When we are present, we savor life.

Make it work for you: Instead of "killing time," being present is about being aware of and focused on what is happening now. The more you zone out or disengage with life the more you develop a pattern of not being present. If you zone out during a class you don't enjoy, you will be more likely to zone out at the pizza place after school when you wanted to hear what your friend was saying. (Try finding something interesting in every situation, even if it's playing a mental game like imagining what the people's lives around you are like when you're stuck in a long line.) Keep track of how often you're zoning out and push yourself to connect to what's happening around you.

The magical side of being present: When you are present, it is easier for you to navigate life. Your intuition will be able to pick up on subtle cues in your environment and from people in your life that help you take a higher or more ideal path. This makes the most of your time on planet earth and allows you to live at your highest potential.

The shadow side of being present: Sometimes we need to take a break from life—from family drama, war, natural disasters, college applications, final exams, neighborhood violence, friendship conflicts. The key is to find a balance where you are present enough to understand your situation and take action, but removed enough to maintain your emotional stability and sense of grounding.

Give it a try: List five activities in your journal that you engage in that are not always healthy escapes (like gossiping), or maybe they can be healthy but you tend to overuse them (like complaining). Try to replace some of these with a healthier escape or use them more in moderation.

Tips and tricks:

1. Remember that it might be hard to be fully present when something very upsetting or traumatic is happening. This is when it can help to take life in small doses or bites. Make sure you have plenty of space in your schedule to take healthy escape breaks, like hanging out with friends or getting lost in a great book.
2. Have a conversation with someone and really listen or be present to what they are saying, instead of thinking of when you can jump in and talk or zoning out.
3. Go out to lunch with friends and have a no-phone zone for an hour. Unless someone is expecting urgent news, turn the phones off and be fully present with each other.
4. Ask yourself how you are feeling. Sometimes we might not be present to the fact that we are happy or sad—or any shade in between—until we ask ourselves that question.

5. Let it be okay to make mistakes. Instead of running from, justifying, or hiding a mistake, just own up to it or be present with yourself and anyone else involved. Learn from the experience and move on—mistakes happen all the time.

6. Avoid caffeine and sugar. These two can make you feel racy or revved up before crashing your system. Being present means being able to pay attention and experience even energy throughout the day.

7. Take your time. If the day felt like it whizzed by, you probably were not that present.

8. Do less, experience more. This is a fabulous mantra if you are in the market for one! Instead of cramming your schedule with activities and responsibilities, create some space in your days so you can actually be present and savor what you are doing.

9. Engage your five physical senses. Do things that engage you on a touch, taste, smell, hearing, and seeing level to stay more present.

10. Take a break with nature. Fifteen or twenty minutes walking in nature without listening to music or talking on the phone can help you better remain present the rest of the day.

31

Express Challenging Emotions

Why it works: It takes great effort to keep negative emotions bottled up, and expressing them gives you relief—it's like putting down a heavy object you have been carrying in an awkward position for too long.

Disappointment, frustration, anger, sadness, fear, loneliness, and regret can be difficult to experience, yet they must be experienced. If we do not process our challenging emotions, they don't go away. They sit in our systems and wait to be processed, just like your dirty laundry does not go away if you ignore it. The laundry simply piles up and gets worse—and might even start to smell or take over your whole house. (Can laundry develop a personality? Don't find out.) But seriously, you don't have to be afraid of your more challenging or negative emotions. Try to make friends with them. After all, they are a part of you. And expressing these emotions is like doing your laundry—refreshing! So if you ignore your anxiety or embarrassment, you are really ignoring yourself. Remember, it's normal for all humans to experience challenging emotions on a regular basis.

Think of sitting with these emotions as a healing experience. It's a great chance for self-nurturing by accepting all of yourself.

Sitting with these emotions makes you feel safer, because once you acknowledge them and process them, they won't seem so overwhelming or terrible. And the sooner you start processing these emotions the sooner they will pass, just like a thunderstorm seems intense but then passes and the sun comes out again. Being in touch with all your emotions makes you emotionally intelligent.

A philosophical perspective: Our emotions contain messages and lessons, like little treasure chests. If you open up to these emotions you can get to the interesting stuff inside. Anger might be telling you that someone violated a boundary or that you deserve to be treated better. Sadness over a close friend moving away might have triggered an old wound from when your mother died a few years before, and your intense feelings let you know you still miss your mom so much and that your sadness isn't only about your friend. This could put your friend's departure in perspective and make it seem less sad.

Make it work for you: The key to processing these emotions is to address them as soon as they appear, and work through them slowly. Just like you tell a small child to take small bites when they are learning to eat, it's best to process your negative emotions bite by bite instead of trying to shove a whole meal in your mouth at once. There is only so much we can emotionally process at one time, which is why people who've been through major trauma will still have moments years later where old emotions surface, asking to be experienced, healed, and released.

The magical side of expressing challenging emotions: The more we let ourselves feel emotions like grief, and express them by crying, talking to a friend, journaling, singing, or dancing, the more room we will have to experience a deep joy when something good happens! Because we can only hold so much emotionally at one time, our emotional containers are like those big pretty pitchers you fill with flowers and set on a kitchen windowsill. If our pitcher is full of unprocessed rage, we will not be able to fill that pitcher up with as much love until we have made our way through the anger. Processing and expressing challenging emotions makes space for more positive ones to enter.

The shadow side of expressing challenging emotions: You should feel challenging emotions pass in a few days or weeks after they are processed and expressed, or at least start to get breaks where you feel happy and carefree again. If you are having trouble processing a challenging emotion, have been through a major trauma like the loss of an immediate family member, an emotion like depression seems to have settled over you like a dark cloud that won't blow away, or expressing your anger by yelling into a pillow or venting to a friend actually makes you even more angry, don't be afraid to ask for help from people you trust and healthcare professionals. It's normal that sometimes in life we need help working through tough emotions.

Give it a try: Here's how you can work through some common challenging emotions:

> **Grief:** Time really is a great healer. If you wonder if grief over the loss of something or someone will ever pass, you're not alone. Many grieving people have felt this way and learned that grief gets much easier and loses intensity with time. Grief demands patience with ourselves and our emotions. Let your heart grieve and balance that grief with whatever brings you joy.

Disappointment: This emotion really needs to be expressed. Give yourself a few days or even weeks to be upset, mope around, feel sorry for yourself, and soak up love and encouragement from friends and family. Then remind yourself that there are always other opportunities and relationships waiting for you on the other side of disappointment. Hope is a great balancing force for disappointment!

Loneliness: Admitting that you are lonely can be hard, because you may be afraid there is nothing you can do about it. That's not true! Loneliness can also become a pattern that needs to be broken. Remind yourself that you are a really fun, kind, cool, interesting person others would love to be around. Work on your confidence, which should come from within and is not dependent on outside forces. And then start putting yourself out there! Volunteer at an animal shelter, join a book club or other group, take a class and introduce yourself to a couple of people, ask someone to hang out on the weekend, sign up for a sports team. Animals can be great companions and cures for loneliness. If you are very shy, ask for help overcoming social anxiety.

Fear: Most of the things we are afraid of will never happen or never turn out as badly as we fear. Often our imaginations get the best of us with this emotion and make fear much larger than it needs to be. To put your fears in perspective, be honest with yourself and don't try to be brave or pretend you are not afraid. Then talk to a wise, gentle person about your fears. Often when we start talking about our fears out loud they naturally subside. You can also write about your fears in your journal to gain insight. Getting in touch with your inner warrior (pages 113–124) will help you face genuine challenges causing fear. Fear can also be a warning trying to keep you safe, like if you are afraid to do something that is physically dangerous that someone else is teasing or shaming you into trying. That fear should be listened to and respected! As you age, you'll get better at deciding what fears need to be heeded and what fears need to be faced and pushed through.

Embarrassment/shame: It's natural to feel embarrassed occasionally about something you did or said, but don't let that turn into shame. Try laughing about what happened or try to see the humor in it. If there was nothing funny about what happened then treat yourself like a little bird with a broken wing. Be gentle, take some quiet time alone, and heal yourself with your favorite people, food, and activities. The things we are embarrassed about are usually quickly forgotten by others—we are often the ones who keep remembering.

Frustration: This is one of those intense emotions that begs to be expressed before it can settle down, like a volcano needs to erupt or a zit needs to pop—gross, but an accurate comparison. Find healthy ways to express your frustration—exercising, sighing or even yelling, cleaning the house, or writing about your frustration in your journal. This should provide some relief. Then move away from the situation—put your energy somewhere else for a while.

Anger: Sometimes anger can be scary because we do not know how to process it. Often a sadness or depression that will not go away might really be anger waiting to be processed. If you are angry at someone, you can always write them a note letting it all out, and then tear the note into a bazillion little pieces. (That's right, a *ba*zillion.) Or you could get a nice big fluffy pillow and hit it to get some anger out. You might let yourself "go off" to a neutral third party who is not involved in the situation to release some of your anger and get their perspective. Perhaps a good cleansing cry is also in order!

Jealousy: This can be a tough one. Challenging emotions can overlap, so you might have some anger and sadness mixed in with the jealousy. But back to jealousy. Get clear on what you are jealous about: another person's hair, boyfriend, car, health, money, family, talent? Jealousy might be telling you that you want more or different things in your life than what is there right now. See how you might bring some of what this person has into your life. Then find reasons they might be jealous of you! Everyone has amazing and challenging stuff in their lives—it's just that no two lives ever look alike. If you are jealous of someone's talents, it might be that you have hidden talents (we've all got talents) that you haven't tapped into or that are not being recognized by others.

Regret: It can be a very healthy thing to feel regret. This emotion lets you know when something was more important to you than you realized or that you would handle something differently if you could go back in time. Well, you cannot go back in time, but you can do things differently in the future. If you're feeling regret, look for the lesson. Part of processing and healing this emotion is forgiving yourself. You are always worthy of forgiveness, no matter what you have done. We've all made mistakes, sometimes big ones and sometimes small ones. But you will get other chances to make better decisions in the future.

The next time you feel a challenging emotion trying to get your attention, don't move away from it by pretending you are not upset, keeping your feelings to yourself, or trying to distract yourself from your feelings with work, excessive exercise, video games, or food. Relax and let yourself go with the flow of your emotions and see where that takes you. Trust that you can handle or get help for any emotion that comes up.

32

Seek out Simple Pleasures

Why it works: You've probably heard people say, "It's the little things," when describing what brings them joy. Simple pleasures are either free or cheap, and they remind us why we enjoy being alive. The daily grind of responsibilities and chores can weigh anyone down, but sitting outside and watching the sunset, holding someone's hand, sipping a warm cup of your favorite something on a cold morning, playing with a pet, holding a baby, or sleeping in under comfy covers keeps us grateful to be in the middle of space on this rotating orb called Earth.

A philosophical perspective: Just like there is a recommended daily allowance of certain foods and vitamins, you should have a recommended daily allowance of simple pleasures. Pleasure feeds the soul, and our souls need to be fed daily, just like our bodies and minds.

Make it work for you: Incorporating simple pleasures into your life can change your life dramatically. Sometimes it's the simple things that make the largest impact on our happiness. Try to work in three simple pleasures a day, and see if you feel calmer and more positive about your life!

The magical side of simple pleasures: These simple pleasures can make us realize that we don't need so much to be happy. Maybe chasing a fancier car, a different house, or a bigger wardrobe aren't always authentic paths to happiness. Simple pleasures can curb your urge to fill a void in your life with consumerism—which can leave you unhappy and broke.

The shadow side of simple pleasures: Try not to get too attached to any one simple pleasure. If you are dead set on holding someone's hand and you end up spending the afternoon alone, it will only bum you out. In this case, there will be another day to hold someone's hand. Snuggle with a pet or curl up with a great book instead.

Give it a try: Challenge yourself to enjoy at least one simple pleasure each day, like getting yourself fresh flowers, hanging out with a friend, taking a nap, going for a run, or listening to your favorite musical artist. Try to be present and mindful as you experience this simple pleasure to enjoy the full benefits. See if this makes you feel blissed out or more content!

Tips and tricks:

Eat a small piece of dark chocolate (the healthiest kind) and really savor it, letting each small bite melt in your mouth. (If you are sensitive to milk or sugar you can find chocolate sweetened with stevia or made of almond milk, or you can indulge in some other small, rich, but affordable delicacy.) Eating a tiny bit of something sweet reinforces that you don't have to have a lot of something to feel satisfied.

Do something that makes you feel free with the wind whipping your hair or face. Examples: riding a bike, riding a horse, riding in your wheelchair, going for a brisk walk or jog, dancing, doing yoga somewhere outside like on your porch or on the beach, riding in a car with the windows down.

Make a new friend. If there is someone at work, at school, or in your neighborhood who is your age and seems interesting, ask them out to lunch.

Celebrate something. We all have reasons to celebrate that we often neglect. Maybe you just finished a project or finished a grade or just powered through a really rough day when you were feeling beat. Treat yourself to something special to celebrate this big or mini milestone, like buying an aromatherapy candle or lying in the grass and daydreaming the afternoon away.

Sing out loud. If you have to clean the house or do some other type of chore, put on your headphones or crank up your tunes and sing along to your favorite album— dancing is allowed, too! This is how simple pleasures can make something that seems un-fun suddenly super fun. It doesn't matter if you're a great singer or not.

continues

Tips and tricks *continued*

Challenge yourself. Set a goal for yourself—a really simple one like learning a piece of music that is a bit difficult or mastering a tough, thousand-piece puzzle. You can work on this piece of music or puzzle a little bit every day alone or with a friend. Accomplishing something just for fun can actually be very pleasurable and boost your self-confidence.

Read about a subject that fascinates you. Are you a foodie? A fashionista? A budding spiritual guru? The next big fantasy writer? Stop by the local library or bookstore and spend some time browsing in your favorite section. Pick up a book or two and dive in. Learning about your passions is a healthy addiction.

Try something new with your body. Have you always been curious about hiking or yoga or Pilates or rowing but never given it a go? There are classes with qualified instructors on almost everything these days, and most are pretty inexpensive. You might stumble on a hobby that keeps you happy *and* in shape. If you have a physical limitation or injury, don't feel left out. Look for a unique class, instructor, or activity that is just right for you!

Let a friend give you a silly makeover. Allow someone else to pick out your clothes or do your makeup just for fun. Try something new and don't be too serious when you look in the mirror. If the result is kind of cool but also makes you laugh, you nailed it!

Tell someone you love them. It might be a best friend, a close family member, or your main romantic squeeze, but letting someone know you care deeply for them will release a bunch of feel-good endorphins in both your systems. That's *amore*!

33

Accept What's Beyond Your Control

W hy it works: There are some things in life that are out of your control. Having a friend, loved one, or pet pass; watching your parents get divorced; and being rejected by your crush or boyfriend/girlfriend are all experiences that can make you feel helpless because you can't control the outcome of these situations. Witnessing a friend spiral into addiction or not getting into your college of choice can also be out of your control. You might have urged your friend to get help and even told an adult you trusted about the situation and nothing seemed to change. Perhaps you gave 110 percent of yourself to the application process at your dream college and met all the requirements—yet you still did not get into that school.

It can be so valuable in life to get better at recognizing situations you truly have no or limited control over. One important thing to remember is that we can never control another person. We can try to persuade, educate, or influence other people, but each of us has a free will that we can exercise at any time.

A philosophical perspective: Occasionally a situation will seem within our control . . . and then, as time passes, we realize we don't have as much control as we thought. Healing journeys are great examples. You might have had an injury, and the doctors told you that with physical therapy you will make a complete recovery. So you dedicate yourself to your therapy, working hard. But then a complication arises. While you do recover it's not exactly the "complete" recovery the doctors assured you of. You did everything you were supposed to, but it turns out that this situation was not completely in your control.

Make it work for you: Life has so many variables that, when you think about it, not much is completely within our control—except perhaps the way we choose to view or approach a situation. Instead of letting a lack of control make you feel angry or frustrated, allow it to be liberating. Maybe you don't have to be perfect. Maybe you can just relax, do your best, and then release the outcome. After all, only so much is within your control. Realizing that you don't have full control over much in life can make you adopt a more easygoing attitude to this earthly adventure you are on. And remember that concept of grace from earlier in the book? Grace really kicks in when you don't have much control over something, so look for life to send you helpful people, knowledge, and opportunities out of the blue that will make this situation better.

The magical side of accepting things beyond your control: This shift of accepting that some things are beyond your control can be excellent at helping you see when to try and how much you should try. Once you get good at recognizing what degree of control you have over a situation, you will find yourself wasting less time and energy.

The shadow side of accepting things beyond your control:
Don't use this as an excuse not to try, or give your best to something. Many times you play a large part in the outcome of situations in your life. Even if you don't have complete control, often you do have some partial control that will affect the quality of the outcome.

Give it a try:

Step 1. Identify some situations in your life where you have no control (the eye color you were born with, for example).

Step 2. Identify some situations in your life where you have limited control (like whether you become a famous filmmaker or not).

Step 3. Now think about how you want to mentally and emotionally approach these situations differently in the future. Maybe you want to practice looking at situations in your life or goals for the future to analyze just how much control you will have over the outcome. This is a good way to flex your strategy muscles.

Tips and tricks:

1. **Take a step back from the situation and go away from it for a while.** This will help you gain perspective and discover what is within your control as well as your next best action step.

2. **Forgive yourself.** Sometimes realizing we have limited or no control over a situation helps us to be less judgmental of ourselves. So give yourself a break for any "mistakes" you think you might have made—you were not in complete

control of this situation anyway and the outcome to situations is rarely in your complete control.

3. **Talk it out.** Speak to someone you love and trust about your feelings around this situation. Sometimes just talking it out, even if talking won't change anything, can make you feel a lot better. Talking to someone who is gentle, kind, and a good listener is always productive.

4. **Prepare for the worst.** Thankfully the worst rarely happens. But if you accept that the worst-case scenario could happen ahead of time, you will feel more calm if it happens. Sometimes thinking about the worst-case scenario makes us realize what a slim chance there is that the worst will happen.

5. **Get support.** Whatever is going on, get the support of friends, loved ones, bosses, coworkers, teachers, and health-care providers. One thing you can control is your willingness to ask others for their assistance and support.

6. **Stop fighting it.** Sometimes there are action steps we can take to help resolve or influence a situation, and other times we just need to accept the outcome. It takes a lot of energy, strength, and willpower to fight something. Only fight for something if you still have a chance of changing or influencing a situation. Otherwise begin to move on.

7. **Decide what your attitude will be.** There is a saying that the only thing in life you can control is your attitude. You can't always control the outcome of a situation, or even your emotions around a situation, but you might decide to take on a hopeful attitude, a look-on-the-bright-side attitude, a proactive attitude, a surrendering attitude, a humble attitude, or an attitude of gratitude.

34

Find Your Soul Tribe

Why it works: Feeling like you are tackling life alone can be silently stressful. Humans are pack animals, and just having a few soul friends you can lean on and laugh with will make life seem safer and calmer.

Some brothers and sisters you were born with, and others you pick up along the way. Have you ever met someone and felt like they were always a part of your life or like you had always known them although you just met? Maybe you gravitate to this person and you two spend a lot of your free time together. Or it might be that this person lives far away, but they are never far away from your thoughts or heart. Soul friends feel familiar and comforting—they feel like home.

Soul friends always want the best for you, even if they sometimes challenge you or pick a fight. Soul friends are loyal, and no matter your differences you know these friends always have your back. Soul friends are often people you share a mutual passion with, like a love of sports or music or spirituality or books or activist causes or animals or humor. You know someone is a soul friend when it's hard to imagine your life without them.

A philosophical perspective: Why might you think of these special people as "soul" friends? Because your connection to them is not surface level. It goes much deeper, to the soul level. The concept of the soul is really the concept of our true self, and these soul friends love, accept, and appreciate our true selves. We always think of the term "soul mate" as describing a romantic relationship. But friends can be soul mates too! Soul friends don't come around every day. So when you find one . . . try to hang on to them! Soul friends might disappoint you or get mad at you from time to time, but be prepared to give or receive an apology. Soul friends are often in it for the long haul. Although some soul friends are really meant to be in our lives for only a certain time or only in a certain place. Just because you and a soul friend both move on and lose contact does not mean the love is gone or that the friendship wasn't deep.

Make it work for you: If you have a soul friend who moves to a different town or goes to a college on the other side of the country, try to stay in touch. Even emailing or talking on the phone once every few months can keep a friendship alive. If you and a soul friend grow apart, don't worry. Another soul friend will come along. Soul friends know us well, so they can help keep us in check when we aren't at our best or are acting in a way that is not true to who we really are on a core level. Soul friends can also bring out the best in us, seeing where we have untapped talent and potential and encouraging us to go after our dreams.

The magical side of finding your soul tribe: You don't have to have a million friends. Sometimes it's about quality over quantity. Make just one soul friend and you will never truly feel alone.

The shadow side of finding your soul tribe: No one person can be everything to you, so it's great to have different types of friends that you have different things in common with. And remember that soul friendships are not perfect, and you might feel fed up or sick of a soul friend at times. When that happens, take a break from hanging out until you are ready to appreciate your friendship again.

Give it a try:

Step 1. Identify one friend in your life who feels like a soul mate.

Step 2. Write in your journal about why this person feels like a soul mate.

Step 3. Share some of your thoughts with this friend so he or she knows how much you care.

Step 4. Identify someone in your life who you think has the potential to become a soul friend and seek out that person's company in new ways.

35

Ground Yourself in Nature

Why it works: Studies show that nature makes humans feel connected to something larger than themselves, which puts our problems in perspective. A walk in nature is a quick way to alleviate mild bouts of anxiety by reducing your own problems into a smaller, more manageable size.

Nature is healing for the nervous system. Our nervous systems tend to match the energy around us, so taking a break from the hustle and bustle of modern life and all its digital distractions and replacing that with trees, fresh air, and creatures from the animal kingdom can be immensely soothing.

Nature is grounding, and when we are grounded we feel calm and strong. Whether you're soaking in the sun (wear a hat and put on a healthy sunscreen), enjoying a walk through the cloudy mist, or bundling up in a winter wonderland of ice and snow, if your life is fast paced or there has been a lot of drama around you lately, your nervous system will benefit from the steady, usually predicatable rhythm of nature.

A philosophical perspective: When you are in nature, try to match your energy to the energy of the trees, flowers, rivers, sky, grass, and rocks around you. Let your heartbeat slow down. Let your mind go blank or settle. Take a few deep, grounding breaths to center yourself in your physical body, and tune into the flow of nature. Leaves fall and flowers bloom . . . but all in their own sweet time.

Make it work for you: Getting out into nature where you are surrounded by sand, trees, water, meadows, or mountains is ideal. But even having smaller reminders of nature in your home, like a houseplant, fresh flowers, a miniature indoor fountain, or a crystal or other natural stone can also assist you in using nature to calm yourself. Listening to nature sounds, like rainfall or birdsong, can be especially calming after a busy day or right before bedtime.

The magical side of grounding yourself in nature: The effects are often immediate, it's free, and nature is all around you—even if you live in a big city. You don't have to spend all day in nature to get the benefits of resetting your nervous system by grounding in nature. Just a fifteen-minute stroll or lounge outside can relax your body and clear your mind.

The shadow side of grounding yourself in nature: It's easy for city people to forget nature is available to them. If you live in a place that doesn't have a lot of trees, or if it's too hot or cold to go outside, find other ways to experience the natural world: Watch a documentary on nature; listen to nature sounds, like crickets chirping; eat a big, fresh, organic salad with greens and veggies; volunteer at a community or botanical garden; recycle or compost to feel closer to nature; and keep pictures of nature around your home.

Give it a try: Go outside and tune into the energy of a tree, flower, cloud, rock, body of water, leaf, or even a simple blade of grass. You can do this by sitting or standing still and focusing on the object you are tuning into in a relaxing way. Examine the object's physical details, like the veins in a leaf or the sap oozing from a tree. Also pay attention to what you smell and hear.

Tips and tricks for letting nature soothe your soul:

Mountains: If you live close enough to see mountains, drive through them, or even sit at their feet, tuning into mountain energy might make you feel strong and sturdy. If you've had a lot of changes in your life recently, or you feel uncertain about the future, working with mountain energy can make you feel more stable, as mountains are so enormous and fixed (people always joke about how you cannot "move mountains") and have been around for longer than humans could comprehend. Don't live near mountains? You can always look at images of them online or print one out to put on your vision board.

Rivers and streams: Rushing water is so determined. Despite the rocks or trees in their path, rivers and streams find a way to keep moving forward. Even after going over a cliff as a waterfall, water regroups and keeps going again. If you are having trouble going forward with a challenge regarding your health, a relationship, work, or school, or with going forward with a dream or goal, sit by a river or stream where the water is really moving. You can also listen to the sound of running water on a nature sounds radio station or on YouTube. Just like that water, you will find a way forward past your challenges or toward your dreams.

Flowers: These delicate, delightful examples of nature encourage us to bloom and show the world how unique and beautiful we are. There are so many different types of flowers that come in all shapes and sizes and colors. People are just as varied. Do you possess some talents you want to explore and share with the world? If you need encouragement to blossom, go buy some fresh flowers and put them on display in your home. Flowers bloom in their own time, and you, too, will find that your gifts begin to unfold like the petals of a flower at the precisely right moment.

Lakes and ponds: These bodies of water can teach us a lot about stillness. Have you ever been to a smaller body of water first thing in the morning? It's amazing how still a lake or pond can be, even if a family of ducks is paddling across or a fish jumps out of the water to try and catch a bug. These occurrences just seem to cause the smallest ripples, and do not disturb the overall stillness of the scene. Sometimes humans need to be still, too—like when you lie on the couch and read a book undisturbed for an hour, or when you sit in meditation for twenty minutes, or sit outside and watch the sunset with a friend. If life has felt awfully busy lately, imagine the stillness of a pond and try to find some of that same stillness in your life. You experience more deep, insightful, ah-ha thoughts when you cultivate stillness!

Trees: Have you ever read artist/poet Shel Silverstein's book *The Giving Tree*? Although it's a children's book, no one is too old for its message. Trees can teach us a lot about giving. These mighty plants give so much to us: wood to make homes with, to turn into paper we can write on, and to burn to keep us warm—to name just a few. Like trees, each human has a lot to give. But do you ever give away too much? Are you always giving at home or to your friends to the point that you get run-down or irritable? There is a huge movement now to recycle paper products and conserve trees. Humans are realizing that without trees the world would not be such a healthy or beautiful place. Sometimes there are limits to our resources, just like the tree has limited resources. If you need to give away less and spend more time on self-care, go outside and sit under a tree or lay your hand flat against its bark. This will help you connect with tree energy and encourage you to take better care of yourself. It might make you want to help conserve trees, too.

Hills and Valleys: Life sure has its ups and downs, doesn't it? If you've ever walked in a hilly area, you know the peaks and valleys are a great metaphor for life. Hills and valleys can remind us that if we are having a tough time, or in a valley, if we just keep putting one foot in front of the other in life pretty soon we will be on top again, staring out from the vantage point of a lovely grassy hill. Good times and bad times in life have one thing in common—they are both temporary. Savor that feeling when you are on top of the world. And if you're stuck in a valley or feeling you've hit a bottom, know that in time you will feel the exact opposite once again. If you live in a hilly area and are looking for perspective on a difficult or sad time in your life, you might hike to the top of a hill. It takes some effort getting there, but once you do the view is awesome and you can sit down and rest. Kind of like when you have to hike through a tough time or work hard on a goal—it's always worth it in the end. Or you could go online and watch a video of a bird flying or a human hang gliding over a hilly area. Sometimes bird's eye is the best perspective on life!

Wind: Feeling a gentle wind through your hair or against your face can be exhilarating. The wind seems to go where it

pleases when it pleases with no thought of anything or anyone else. That's why many people associate the wind with
freedom or the call to adventure! If you have been feeling
bogged down by life's many responsibilities, you might take
a cue from the wind and be more playful. Think of how the
breeze makes wind chimes jingle or helps boats sail through
the water. Taking a walk or bike ride outside during a mild
wind is a great way to give yourself a break from chores
at home, work, or school. Too much of a good thing can
be bad though, and wind is no exception. Too much wind
causes destructive storms, just like too much freedom and
too little responsibility can cause chaos in your life. Most
things are best in moderation. Except love—can you ever
have too much of that?

36

Flow with Life's Timing

W hy it works: Timing is not always something you can control, no matter how much you plan and schedule. When something does not happen when you want it to, it can test your stamina and your dreams. These are the occasions that call on you to flow with life's timing, because fighting it will sap you of energy and keep you stuck in frustration.

Do you love sports? Maybe you've been playing basketball, football, hockey, baseball, volleyball, tennis, golf, or soccer since you were a kid, and this season was supposed to be the one where you were a starter, first-string, or star player, but then you fell during practice and hurt your knee, and it might mean that you miss the whole season. You're still on the team, but you'll have to wait until next year to be MVP.

Or maybe you applied to your dream college and spent senior year wearing the official T-shirt and imagining what your new life would be like on the college's campus, and then you get a letter saying you weren't accepted. A counselor at the school suggests that if you go to community college for a year and get your grades up you will be a shoe-in for next year. Again, you'll go to the college of your choice, but not this year.

Do you really want to play this sport or go to this college? If it's right for you and you want it badly enough, it will be worth the wait. Or, if waiting isn't right for you, you can surrender to this situation in a different manner by finding new hobbies and other colleges to apply to. Maybe something different, and even cooler, than what you thought you wanted is out there waiting to be discovered.

Life's timing affects us in profound ways. Parents die young. Friends move away. Big opportunities for success come too early or too late for our own sense of readiness. You might be the second chair trumpet in your school's jazz band. When the first chair moves away, you are suddenly thrust into the spotlight, having to take over all the solos at concerts and competitions. When life's timing leaves you feeling unprepared, give yourself a chance to adjust to the pace and what's currently appearing in your life.

A philosophical perspective: Do we always know when things should or should not happen? Perhaps life has its own clock and its own wisdom and reasoning. Certainly, it can be difficult to find the wisdom in life events that bring us great pain. With these unplanned events, all we can do is look for the opportunities they bring—opportunities to grow, feel, learn, heal, and help others.

Make it work for you: Look for the silver linings during a waiting period. Sitting on the bench for a season might give you the chance to help coach other players. Waiting to get into college could give you the opportunity to improve your transcript. Use any amount of time, even if it feels like too much, wisely. Likewise, when life comes at you too fast—when you don't yet feel ready to step up but life calls on you to do it—remember that you have far more strength and wisdom than you realize, and your dormant talents and abilities will rise to the occasion. Even if a parent dies, you might realize you are naturally nurturing and independent. When a life event comes into your life sooner than you feel ready, be sure to ask for help and support and don't be afraid to admit that you feel in over your head. There's no need to manage life's surprises by yourself.

The magical side of flowing with life's timing:

If it's something good that is coming into your life too soon, try to concentrate on the fact that this is actually a blessing, no matter the timing. If it's something good and you are having to hurry up and wait, the same holds true. Concentrate on the fact that this good thing is still a possibility for you or on the horizon. Try to trust that there is some greater reason, though it may be a mystery now, why life is making you wait or hurry up. If what you are dealing with is a tragedy or a challenge, no matter when it comes, it's going to hurt. Spend a little time counting your other blessings, as remembering what you are still grateful for is very healing.

The shadow side of flowing with life's timing:

Surrendering to the timing of a situation is not an excuse to stop taking action. No matter when a dream or goal happens, it likely won't happen at all if you are not doing your part. And if something happens that is negative, you will need to take time to grieve and process, but eventually you still need to pick yourself up and get back in the game of life. If you ever have trouble doing that, don't feel ashamed. Feeling stuck in a pit of grief quicksand usually happens to everybody at least once in life. Reach out for help from friends, family, teachers, and health-care professionals. If you ever get to a place in life where you cannot help yourself, let people know!

Give it a try:

Step 1. Get out your journal and think back on a time when something seemed to happen too soon or too late.

Step 2. Use the following prompts as a way to explore and learn from this experience in your journal.

How am I proud of some of the ways I handled that situation that seemed to come too soon or too late, or what were some coping skills that worked?

What do I regret, or how would I handle a similar situation—that felt like it happened too soon or too late—differently now?

What were some of the biggest lessons that experience about timing taught me?

How/when did I get support from others, and how/when did I try to be impossibly strong and just go it alone?

What was the scariest or most intimidating part of this unexpected timing experience?

Was there some way in which this unexpected timing experience was easier than I had anticipated?

How was the experience harder than I had anticipated?

What were some of the silver linings or blessings in disguise of this event happening sooner or later than I wanted it to?

What was most comforting to me during this time of change or waiting?

How did I express or honor my emotions?

How did I blow off steam, have fun, find healthy escapes, stay inspired, laugh, or stay connected to others and myself during this period in my life?

Step 3. Identify a situation right now that is inviting you to flow with life's timing.

Step 4. Ask yourself how you are resisting flowing with life's timing, or timing that is out of your control, regarding this situation.

Step 5. Read over your answers to the prompts above, and see how you might apply them to a situation you are currently facing. Ask yourself: "If I were five years older and looking back, how would I have wanted myself to handle this?" What words of comfort or wisdom might you have for yourself?

Tips and tricks:

1. **Unexpected timing is often accompanied by unexpected help and resources.** Along with this unanticipated waiting or action, life will probably throw you a few life preservers in the form of helpful people and surprising opportunities for support. Watch out for these blessings!

2. **When something seems off-schedule, expect some specific and intense emotions.** If an event feels like it's not happening fast enough, you will probably feel disappointed and frustrated. If something feels like it is happening too quickly, you will likely feel scared and anxious. Don't pretend everything is fine. Cry or allow yourself to get angry. Also make sure you have someone understanding to talk to. Journaling can be very helpful for making sense of and exploring your emotions.

3. **Remember that the bigger this change is, the more support from others you will need.** Don't try to be a hero and go it alone. Think of all the help and sidekicks heroes have!

4. **Allow yourself time to adjust to this change.** You might feel a sense of shock or unreality as you psychologically get used to the new normal. Things will settle down and feel natural again in time.

5. **Keep in mind that even "good changes," when they happen before you feel ready, can be stressful, especially in the beginning.** Find ways to blow off steam or manage any anxious feelings. Watch a great comedy or get lost in an activity with a friend.

6. **Identify someone who has gone through a similar experience.** This could be someone in your life or someone famous or in history that you have never met. Reading about or talking to someone who has gone through something similar to your situation will make you feel less alone, give you courage, and might also provide you with some practical insights.

7. **Make room to manage this change.** Whether it's happening too fast or not fast enough, you'll want to give yourself space to deal with this situation. Take some things off your plate if you can.

37

Make Music Playlists with Meaning

W hy it works: Music distracts the mind, putting distance between your mind and stressful thoughts by filling the space with pleasant sonic sensations.

Music is often considered the highest form of art, as just a few notes can dramatically change someone's mood. Think about the creepy music that comes on during a scary scene in a movie and makes you squirm in your seat with anticipation, or the sweet, sentimental song that comes on at the end of a love story and chokes up your throat with feeling. Music is powerful! And it can be a powerful way to change your mood or process your emotions.

If something happened that is making you feel emotional like a romantic breakup, you might create a playlist with all those bittersweet songs that are both happy and sad at the same time. This could help you touch base with your heart and feel all the feelings, while reminding you that this is not the end of the world and that there will be other loves. If you are preparing for a big test like the SAT, you might put together a playlist that inspires you—maybe songs that speak to your inner warrior and get you pumped up and feeling more confident for the big day, like punk or hip-hop. Or maybe tests always make you really anxious, and a soothing playlist of your favorite ballads, folk, or acoustic singer/ songwriter-type stuff would do the trick. You might make a musical playlist for your best friends of songs that you all like or that remind you of each other. A playlist can be a memorable, unique gift.

A philosophical perspective:
Playlists can also become a record of your life—a musical memoir. You might pull up a playlist from a few years ago and have each song bring back memories from that time. There are almost no rules to creating these playlists, so it's a perfect way to express yourself. Completely your call about what goes on a playlist, and how many things in life are completely up to you? Not as many as you might like! That's why playlists can be a great stress reliever.

Make it work for you:
Think of your playlists as a creative project. After all, it's almost like you are making your own unique musical composition. Choosing the order of the songs, the theme, and the title of the playlist (like "Rainy Day Tunes Playlist" or "All Psyched Up Playlist") are very creative endeavors.

The magical side of making playlists with meaning:
Ever wish your life had a soundtrack? With today's artists and technology, you can actually design one. Your story, or your life, is the most fascinating and important story you will ever witness—it deserves some killer tunes.

The shadow side of making playlists with meaning:
If you have outgrown a playlist, just put it aside and create something new. It can be easy to fall into a rut, so don't let that happen with your music playlists! Ask friends who their favorite artists are for inspiration.

Give it a try: You guessed it! Make a new playlist with a specific theme and cool name. Try to use an interesting mix of artists and types of music, and have fun with the order. Don't limit your list to songs that are already in regular rotation: get experimental! You might enjoy some of the song suggestions on pages 197–200. Hashtag #ZenTeen to share your playlist!

You can tailor your playlists to suit your moods. Make playlists to listen to when:

You feel like celebrating, like after you pass your driver's test or score an internship.

You feel sentimental about the past, like when a friend moves away or you hit a milestone like graduation.

You are angry about something that happened, like when a friend hurts your feelings, someone at home disappoints you, or you're upset about world events.

You need healing, like when someone you love passes away or you want to heal a self-sabotaging pattern.

You feel inspired, like when you set a goal for yourself or stretch yourself beyond your known limits.

You feel grateful, like when an unexpected blessing comes your way or you just feel happy to be alive.

You feel sad, like when something does not turn out the way you hoped or your heart hurts for a friend going through a hard time.

You feel excited, because something amazing like your first day of college is coming up or you just got your first real boyfriend or girlfriend.

You want to chill, because you have been busting your butt at school or work, or life at home has gotten too heavy lately.

ZEN PLAYLISTS:
TUNES FOR EVERY MOOD

Punk

**Connect with your inner rebel and question
the status quo or conventional wisdom.**

The Ramones, "I Believe in Miracles"

Bleached, "Dead in Your Head"

Fugazi, "Waiting Room"

The Specials, "Enjoy Yourself"

Siouxsie & the Banshees, "Kiss Them for Me"

Tacocat, "Talk"

Hip-Hop

Claim your personal power or just get your groove on.

Kris Kross, "Jump"

De La Soul, "Me, Myself and I"

Outkast, "Hey Ya"

Beastie Boys, "Lighten Up"

TLC, "Don't Go Chasing Waterfalls"

Lauryn Hill, "Everything Is Everything"

Kirk Franklin, "I Smile"

Pop

Take a break, get inspired, and have some fun.

B.E.R., "The Night Begins to Shine"

Jill Scott, "Golden"

Katy Perry, "Roar"

Chromatics, "Running up That Hill"

Madonna, "Express Yourself"

Michael Jackson, "Rock with You"

Walk the Moon, "Shut Up and Dance"

Cyndi Lauper, "True Colors"

Lady Gaga, "Born This Way"

Daft Punk, "Lose Yourself to Dance"

Eurythmics and Aretha Franklin, "Sisters Are Doin' It for Themselves"

Icona Pop, "Brightside"

Christian Burghardt, "Safe Place to Land"

Rachel Platten, "Fight Song"

Pharrell Williams, "Happy"

World Music

Experience a different culture to get out of your own head.

Loreena McKennitt, "Night Ride Across the Caucasus," Canada

Björk, "Come to Me," Iceland

Bob Marley, "Three Little Birds," Jamaica

Tame Impala, "Feels Like We Only Go Backwards," Australia

Enya, "May It Be," Ireland

Bomba Estéreo, "Soy Yo," Colombia

Kailash Kher, "Chak Lein De," India

Rock

Be cool and claim your independence.

Alabama Shakes, "Hang Loose"
The Stone Roses, "She Bangs the Drum"
The Beatles, "Here Comes the Sun"
Fleetwood Mac, "Don't Stop"
David Bowie, "Heroes"
Lenny Kravitz, "Let Love Rule"
The Go-Go's, "Our Lips Are Sealed"
Free Energy, "Free Energy"
Jimi Hendrix, "Voodoo Child"
Imagine Dragons, "On Top of the World"

Classical

Appreciate the finer things to ground yourself.

Chopin, nocturnes
Vitamin String Quartet, "Don't Stop Believing"
Beethoven, Symphony No. 9
Taylor Davis, "Star Wars Medley"

Jazz

Feel wild and free and explore the magic of creativity.

Miles Davis, "So What"
Kamasi Washington, "Truth"
The Hot Sardines, "Bei Mir Bist Du Schoen"
Nina Simone, "Feeling Good"

Singer/Songwriter & Folk Music

Connect with your heart and the beauty of self-expression.

10,000 Maniacs, "These Are Days"
The Wailin' Jennys, "Arlington"
Mac DeMarco, "Treat Her Better"
The Lumineers, "Scotland"
The Grateful Dead, "Ripple"
Bob Dylan, "Mr. Tambourine Man"
Ed Sheeran, "All of Our Stars"
Birdy + Rhodes, "Let It All Go"
Neil Young, "Helpless"
k.d. lang, "Hallelujah"
MaMuse, "Glorious"
Kate Wolf, "Across the Great Divide"

Country

Get in touch with the simpler things and keep it real.

Willie Nelson, "Blue Eyes Cryin' in the Rain"
Garth Brooks, "Standing Outside the Fire"
Lee Ann Womack, "I Hope You Dance"
Chris Stapleton, "Traveller"
Dixie Chicks, "Lullaby"
Luke Bryan, "Most People Are Good"
Dolly Parton, "Coat of Many Colors"

38

Indulge in Beauty Therapy

Why it works: There's an old fable about a homeless man who goes from village to village looking for work. One day he comes across someone who needs his assistance. "If you help me clear out the trash from the back of my store today, I'll give you a silver coin." The homeless man happily agrees, and at the end of a hard day's labor he is given a silver coin, a hot dinner, and a place on the floor to sleep for the night.

The man goes out into the village the next morning with his silver coin. He buys enough bread to get him through the next few days. The man looks down at his palm and realizes he still has a little bit of change left. He sees a flower shop and some yellow daffodils in the window. His heart leaps in his chest and he feels warm all over. For the first time in a long while, he smiles.

This man has a decision to make: Should he save the money for more bread, or should he buy a flower to carry with him on his travels? If he's careful, the man thinks, the flower might last two whole days or more. The man walks into the store and picks out the sweetest bloom.

The moral of the story: Humans get hungry for more than just food—we also crave beauty. It's essential to the human spirit, and the reason we are drawn to art, color, and the brilliance in nature. It's also why certain people devote their lives to creating beauty. People like visual artists, fashion designers, architects, landscapers, jewelry makers, interior decorators, and chefs.

A philosophical perspective: Have you ever walked into a museum that was exhibiting one of your favorite artists? Do you have a favorite flower or color? Is there a city like Paris, Rome, or New York where you admire the architecture? Is there a forest, beach, or desert whose beauty takes your breath away? All of these are dramatic examples of beauty, and the expansive, inspiring, pleasurable feeling you get when you are surrounded by beauty is the point of beauty therapy. Remember that beauty is subjective, so what you find beautiful, your friend might find forgettable.

Make it work for you: Once you become more sensitive to beauty you will notice it in more subtle ways, such as on your phone case or the cover of your journal—or even in a plant growing up from a crack in the sidewalk.

The magical side of beauty therapy: Beauty does not have to be big and it does not have to be expensive. You can seek it out or you can let it reveal itself to you in everyday life.

The shadow side of beauty therapy: Craving beauty can become an obsession, one that makes us spend too much money or care too much about appearances. Look for beauty in unexpected places and unique-looking people, like model Winnie Harlow.

Tips for indulging in beauty therapy:

Go shopping in your own closet or someone else's. Look in the back of your drawers for clothes you forgot about and then do a clothing swap with a friend.

Become a thrifter. Secondhand and thrift shopping can be a fun way to spend an afternoon and pick up a great vegan leather jacket, vintage concert T-shirt, or a pretty vase without spending a lot of cash.

Dress up old furniture. Sick of looking at the same old desk, nightstand, or dresser in your room? Throw a pretty patterned scarf over it for some color or buy some hand-painted knobs to dress up the front.

Get outside. Plan a day trip with some friends to a natural wonder not far from your hood. Pick a place you've never been to before.

Visit a famous piece of art. Is there a sculpture garden or museum near you? Spend an afternoon there and notice the type of art you personally find most beautiful.

Create a piece of art. Sewing, pottery, painting, drawing, collage, woodworking, graphic design . . . there are tons of media you can explore to make visual art. Find one that calls to you. There's nothing like creating beauty with your own hands. Who knows, maybe you'll be selling your art on Etsy someday!

Write a song. Can you play the guitar, or at least a few chords? Music is great beauty therapy and a fun way to impress yourself and your friends.

Cook a meal. Cooking truly can be an art form. Make something special for yourself and a friend or family member and really take your time with what chefs call "presentation," or

how you arrange the food on the plate and what you use for
garnish and color.

Grow a plant. Get a small succulent or other plant (make sure
you read up about the right conditions to help it grow) and
tend it in your room or garden. The beauty of plants brings
a lot of affordable joy.

Look for sales. Certain times of year will find stores and sites
offering their best bargains. You might have to wait for
something you want to go on sale, but the extra money left
in your pocket will be worth it.

Give it a try: Challenge yourself to bring more beauty into your
life while noticing the overlooked beauty that has been there all
along. Use the following journal prompts for guidance:

1. Things about myself that are beautiful.
2. Clothes/shoes in my wardrobe I love.
3. Items in my room I always like to look at.
4. My favorite places in nature.
5. Artistic styles I dig.
6. I can bring more beauty to the world by . . .

39

Treat Your Body as a Temple

W hy it works: Taking great care of your body will shore up your physical and emotional reserves and boost resiliency.

Many people like to view the body as the physical container for things that are not physical or cannot be touched—like the soul or the personality of an individual. And what a physical container it is! The human body is like the finest, most complex machine ever built. Even modern computers pale in comparison to the design of organs like the brain, liver, and lungs.

One way to begin treating your body as a temple, or something sacred, is to make friends with it—and we do this through loving acceptance. We all have things we sometimes would like to change about our bodies. Maybe you occasionally wish you were taller or shorter. It's normal to sometimes wish our bodies were different. But if that occasional daydream turns into a constant yearning, it can be self-sabotaging and even dangerous. No matter what you do or don't like about your body, work on accepting and loving it.

A philosophical perspective: Treating the body as a temple is about respecting, loving, and appreciating your body. Your relationship with your body is one of the most important relationships you will ever have, because your body has been with you from the beginning of this life and it will be with you until the end of this life. Every body will have different limits and requirements. Get to know your unique body well, and that will help you honor and meet its needs.

Make it work for you: What if there are things about your body beyond hair color or size you would like to change? What if you were born blind, or with only one arm? You would still survive, and even thrive. Stevie Wonder and Ray Charles were blind, and they became musical stars. Beethoven was deaf, and he was one of the most famous composers of all time. And the drummer for rock band Def Leppard lost an arm in a car accident and still went on to tour the world with his band. Amy Purdy lost both her legs as a teen and went on to be a professional athlete, actress, model, author, and inspirational speaker (she even wowed the nation on *Dancing with the Stars*—check it out on YouTube). Let your body serve you by focusing on your gifts, not your limitations.

The magical side of treating the body as a temple: The more you honor your body, the more you will be able to recognize and utilize its special gifts. Once loving acceptance of the body has begun, your comfort in your own skin will increase, and so will your confidence.

The shadow side of treating the body as a temple: It's fine to want to improve the body, like working out to be more fit or playing around with makeup to enhance your features. But changing our bodies can become an unhealthy obsession, and obsession is a form of anxiety.

Tips for treating your body as a temple:

Stay away from foods and drinks that are unhealthy or ones that you have a particular sensitivity to (such as dairy or gluten).

Unless you are training to be a professional athlete, exercise in moderation.

Compliment your body every now and again, like thinking, "Wow, I loved the way my body owned the dance floor at the party on Saturday" or "Man, I'm really starting to get some serious definition in my arms" or "I was so proud of my body for making it through that physical therapy session."

Get enough rest. If you had a busy week, catch up on rest over the weekend.

Drink clean, filtered water. Many filters are very affordable.

Consider investing in an air filter with your family or roommates. This can help remove pet dander, pollution, and germs from your environment.

Walk or ride a bike instead of driving a car when you can. This is great for the body and the planet. Just make sure if you ride a bike that you wear a helmet and stay safe.

Don't skip meals. The body likes to be fed every three to four hours, even if it's just a snack like a banana and some almonds.

Eat organic. Every year it becomes easier to find affordable organic options at the supermarket.

Listen to your body. Often the body will tell you if something is off. If you are having headaches, tummy aches, low energy, or bouts of anxiety, find a health-care professional who can help. You deserve to feel as healthy as you can!

Express yourself and your creativity through your clothes. You do not have to wear expensive clothes to express yourself, but liking what you wear will give your energy and confidence a boost and help you feel more authentic.

Give it a try:

Exercise 1

Identify one or two easy ways you could improve the way you care for your body.

Identify one or two medium or difficult ways you could improve the way you care for your body.

For one week, try to do at least one of the items on your list every day.

Exercise 2

Identify a part of your body that makes you unhappy.

Ask yourself what hidden blessings you might find in this aspect of your body.

Imagine a friend or relative is having the same issue with his or her body: What words of love, comfort, and inspiration would you offer?

Protect the Planet

40

Why it works: There is no way to sugarcoat it: the earth needs your help. There's also no point in sugarcoating things. When you avoid a problem, like pollution in the oceans or dwindling natural resources, it only gets worse. If a problem in the world or your life seems too scary or overwhelming to face, remember there is always hope. Take small, consistent, manageable action steps regarding this problem. That will make you feel much better and will help whatever challenging situation you or the world is up against.

If we're lucky, we each have a home. A real house, apartment, or room where we feel safe and our survival needs (food, shelter, clothing) are met. But beyond our individual homes, everyone on the planet shares the same home—earth. We need to put as much time, thought, and energy into protecting and maintaining the planet as we do our individual dwellings.

A philosophical perspective: There have been people in previous generations who did great harm to the environment unknowingly. Younger generations like you, who are wiser and more informed, have the responsibility of making up for the mistakes of previous generations. But instead of looking at this heavy responsibility as a burden, view it as a gift. Every person reading this book has the chance to be a hero—save the planet, save yourselves, and save each other. Become an environmental "steward," a word that means caretaker. You will be rewarded in your own lifetimes with the beauty and bounty of this planet and also remembered as heroes throughout history.

Make it work for you: The first Earth Day, an annual event that started in 1970, was held on April 22. The event was inspired by the damage caused from a massive oil spill in Santa Barbara and encouraged the public to support a US government–led Environmental Protection Agency. Do something special for the planet on April 22, like remind people on social media how important conservation is, or donate money to an environmentally based nonprofit like the Nature Conservancy. But bear in mind that we need to think of every day as Earth Day. Do something small each day—like pick up a piece of trash off the ground or use mass transit instead of driving a car—to celebrate, honor, and protect our shared home.

The magical side of environmental stewardship: The feeling you get when you give to something that is bigger than yourself is empowering. Taking care of the planet will make you feel more whole, more humble, and more connected to the earth and everyone on it.

The shadow side of environmental stewardship: Caring about the earth can bring about feelings of fear and worst-case-scenario thinking. If you are feeling frightened about the fate of the planet, direct your attention to positive progress: new earth-friendly technologies, organizations saving endangered species, and all the young entrepreneurs who are incorporating environmental stewardship into their business plans.

Tips on how you can be a better steward for the planet:

If you eat meat, join Paul McCartney's Meat-Free Monday campaign, which encourages people to avoid eating meat one day a week. If everyone agreed to stop eating meat for just one day a week, it would have an enormously positive impact on the environment.

Recycle. Most major cities make it easy to recycle and even mandatory to do so. If your town does not yet have a robust recycling program, find out where the nearest drop-off location is and encourage officials in your school, work, and town to recycle.

Look at labels. What ingredients are going into your food, shampoo, soap, deodorant, and makeup? A good rule of thumb is to look for short lists of ingredients with words that you understand or recognize. Unnecessary chemicals pollute the environment.

Pay attention to your waste. Whole Foods stores have signs on their trash. Some say "compost," "recycling," or "landfill." Be very mindful about what you throw away into the garbage that does not go into recycling or composting. Most of it will sit in a landfill for a very long time.

Make a monthly donation. Consider donating as a family or a household to a nonprofit that is dedicated to protecting land, air, water, or wild animals. Even a regular donation of $15 a month adds up.

Purchase paper products made from recycled materials. This is easy now with tons of options. It might cost a few dollars more, but isn't your planet worth it?

continues

Tips on how you can be a better steward for the planet   *continued*

Buy reusable water bottles and coffee/tea mugs. **Have you ever seen a trashcan in a big city filled with plastic water bottles and used coffee cups? What a waste.**

Bring your own bag. **Keep a nylon or cloth bag in your purse or car at all times so that when you buy a few things at a store you don't have to use a plastic bag to carry your items home. Lots of plastic bags end up in the ocean.**

Give it a try: Take an oath to be a better steward of the planet. You can do this exercise by yourself, with a friend, or with your whole family.

Step 1. Go outside on a nice day when there is a gentle wind.

Step 2. Feel the wind on your face or in your hair as you kneel down and put your hand on the earth. Try to find a place where you can actually touch the earth, like placing your hand on soil, grass, sand, or rocks.

Step 3. Close your eyes and tell the earth silently that you will protect it and do your best not to squander its gifts or resources.

Step 4. Spend a few minutes there with your hand touching the earth in silent meditation. Can you feel the earth's energy? Can you feel its gratitude?

ABOUT THE AUTHOR

Tanya Carroll Richardson is a self-improvement/spiritual author, professional intuitive, and regular contributor to Mind BodyGreen.com. Her books include *Angel Intuition*, *Angel Insights*, *Forever in My Heart: A Grief Journal*, *Heaven on Earth*, and *Zen Teen*. Follow Tanya on Instagram at @zenteenchill.